Stump everyone

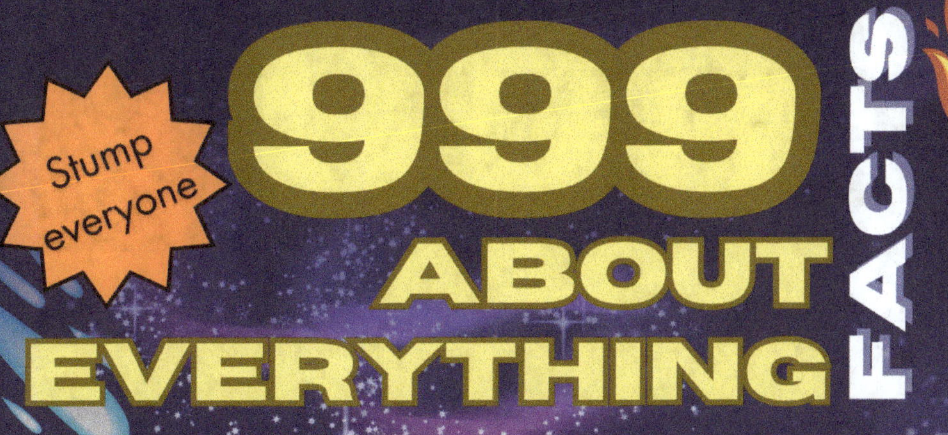

999 FACTS ABOUT EVERYTHING

999 WAYS TO WIN EVERY ARGUMENT
(OR LOSE THEM SPECTACULARLY)

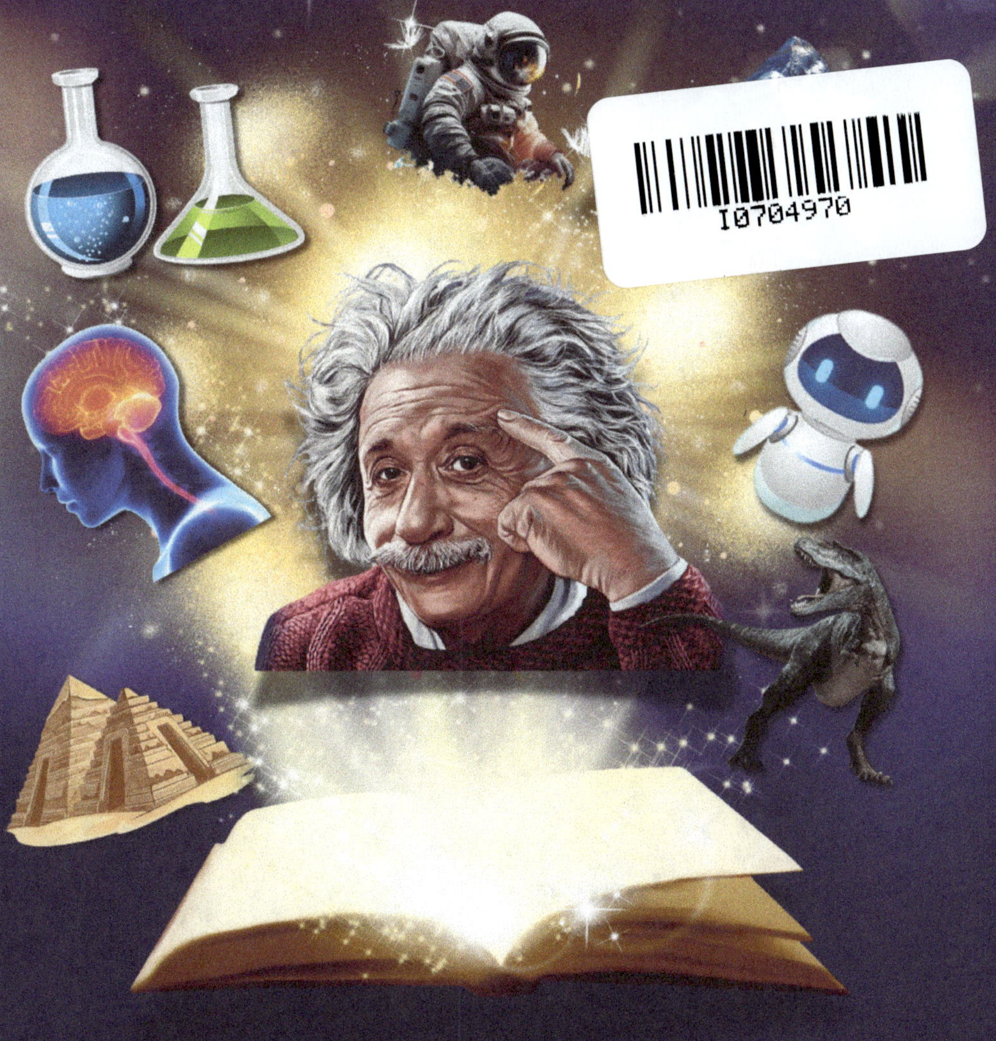

CONTENTS

01

Introduction

02

Facts

- History
- Geography
- Science, physics & technology
- Human's health, features, psychology and behaviors
- Chemistry
- Animal
- Economics, finance, business and marketing
- Film, art, sport & music
- Food & drink
- Cultural traditions, society and laws
- Words & Language

03

Conclusion

INTRODUCTION

elcome to a book that's equal parts fun and fascinating—a treasure trove of facts that will arm you with the ultimate arsenal for any debate, trivia night, or random conversation. Whether you're looking to dazzle your friends with your endless knowledge or simply want to stockpile interesting tidbits to drop at the perfect moment, you've come to the right place.

We've categorized 999 facts into various topics that span the entire spectrum of human knowledge. From the mysteries of history to the quirks of human psychology, from the vastness of space to the intricacies of language, you'll discover facts that are sure to surprise, delight, and maybe even confuse you (in the best way possible).

Ever wanted to know the science behind why your fingers wrinkle in water or the surprising origins of everyday words? Or maybe you're curious about the weirdest laws ever passed or the most peculiar animal behaviors? We've got you covered.

The final part brings everything together in a conclusion that will leave you with a newfound appreciation for the weird and wonderful world we live in. Because if there's one thing this book will prove, it's that the truth really is stranger (and funnier) than fiction.

So buckle up and get ready to dive into 999 facts that will make you laugh, think, and maybe even question reality itself. And remember, whether you win that next argument or lose it in style, you'll have a blast along the way!

HISTORY

1

The Roman-Persian wars are the longest in history, lasting over 680 years. They began in 54 BC and ended in 628 AD.

2

In 1518, a "dancing plague" occurred in Strasbourg, France, where hundreds of people danced uncontrollably for days without rest. Some eventually died from exhaustion or heart attacks. The cause of this phenomenon remains a mystery to this day.

3

Back when dinosaurs existed, there used to be volcanoes that were erupting on the moon.

4

The British government coined the slogan "Keep Calm and Carry on" during World War 2 to motivate citizens to stay strong. Posters with the slogan were printed but never officially issued and were only unearthed in 2000.

5

There was a vampire scare in America in the 19th century where tuberculosis-infected people were thought to be vampires and buried as such. Later exhumations revealed that some of these people were buried with their heads chopped.

6

The youngest Pope in history was Pope Benedict IX, who was either 11 or 20 years old when he was elected in 1032. He is also the only person to have been the Pope more than once.

7

In World War II, Germany tried to collapse the British economy by dropping millions of counterfeit bills over London.

8

Times Square was originally called Longacre Square until it was renamed in 1904 after The New York Times moved its headquarters to the newly built Times Building.

Scotland was one of the few countries able to hold off being conquered by the Romans in the first century A.D.

During WWII, a U.S. naval destroyer won a battle against a Japanese submarine by throwing potatoes at them. The Japanese thought they were grenades.

In the 1830s, the ruler of Egypt, Muhammad Ali Pasha, wanted to disassemble the Giza Pyramids and use them as pre-cut building materials. Thankfully, the Quantity Surveyor for the project fudged the figures and made it look like it would cost too much to save them.

The original London Bridge is now in Arizona. Originally constructed in 1831, the London Bridge began deteriorating in the 1960s, leading the City of London to sell it. In 1963, American entrepreneur Robert P. McCulloch bought and dismantled the bridge, shipping it to Lake Havasu City in Arizona piece by piece. The reconstruction took three years to complete and opened as a tourist attraction on October 10, 1971.

One of the World Trade Centers was built to be 1,776 feet tall on purpose to reference the year the Declaration of Independence was signed.

In 1783, the very first hot air balloon took off with a sheep, a duck, and a rooster on board. A sheep, a duck and a rooster were the first passengers to take a trip in a hot air balloon. The Montgolfier brothers, who invented the hot air balloon, were inspired by their laundry lifting from a fire's heat. The inaugural flight took animal passengers, as it was unknown how flying at high altitudes would affect humans. The animal passengers landed safely, but the sheep ended up on top of the rooster.

15

Humans have been performing dentistry since 7000BC, which makes dentists one of the oldest professions.

16

Sudan has more pyramids than any country, with 255. They outnumber Egyptian pyramids by twice the amount.

17

Six nuclear weapons have disappeared without a trace since the 1950s.

18

During the Second World War, German tank drivers would drive their vehicles over camel droppings, thinking it would bring them good luck.

19

Victorian British ate mummies.

20

A ship was discovered floating in the ocean in 1872, with no signs of its crew or passengers. The ship was called Mary Celeste.

21

In the 1800s, dentures were made from the real teeth of deceased people.

22

Before the invention of cups and bowls, ancient English people used hollowed-out human skulls to hold their food and drink.

23

Before the perfection of cesarean delivery, chainsaws were used to remove parts of the pelvis to allow big babies to pass through the birth canal.

24

There is an ancient book full of bizarre symbols that no one can translate. It's called the Voynich Manuscript.

25

Genghis Khan strategically married off his daughters to expand his empire.
Genghis Khan only gained his title by the time he reached his forties, at which point he had more than ten children. Khan married his daughters to allied kings, who he would send out to war. His new sons-in-law rarely returned alive, and his daughters took control of their new kingdoms for Khan.

26

3% of the population was killed by WWII.

27

The Nazi leader, Hitler, from 1942 until his death in 1945, was addicted to crystal meth.

28

The Titanic wreckage was discovered during a top-secret mission to search for sunken nuclear submarines.

29

There were 42 known assassination attempts on Adolf Hitler.

30

In 897 AD, Pope Formosus was put on trial for perjury and other crimes posthumously.

31

When the Pirates of the Caribbean ride at Disneyland was first built in the 1960s, it used real skeletons.

32

The mummies of Guanajuato, Mexico are believed to have been buried alive. That's due to their dramatic facial expressions.

33

The United States of America's longest-standing unbroken treaty is with Morocco.

34

The 1918 flu pandemic killed even more — between 50 million and 100 million people worldwide.

35

A novel titled "The Wreck of the Titan: Or, Futility" and written 14 years before the sinking of the Titanic ship might have predicted the ship's fate.

36

Ancient Roman commoners went on strike by evacuating their cities, leaving the upper classes hopelessly fending for themselves.

37

17-year-old Willie Francis (January 12, 1929 – May 9, 1947) is the only person to have survived death by electric chair. He survived the ordeal on May 3, 1946 but was eventually executed the following year.

38

During the First World War, so many starving wolves had amassed together in a great pack that opposing German and Russian forces formed a temporary alliance in order to fight them off.

39

People once paid to drink the blood of the recently executed, believing it was healthy.

40

The bubonic plague killed around 75 million people worldwide.

41

The Nazis were the first ever people in modern history to start an anti-smoking and tobacco movement.

42

Spiked and studded dog collars derive from the days of the Ancient Greeks, who would give their sheep-dogs sharply spiked collars to protect their necks from wolves whilst they watched over a Sheppard's flock at night.

43

In Ancient Greece, wearing skirts was manly. In fact, the Ancient Greeks viewed trousers as effeminate and would mock any men who wore them.

44

Augustus Caesar was the wealthiest man to ever live in history. The nephew and heir of Julius Caesar, Roman Emperor Augustus, had an estimated net worth of $4.6 trillion when counting for inflation. Some say that Mansa Musa, king of Timbuktu, was the world's wealthiest man as his wealth was appar

45

For 12 years during the French Revolutionary Period, France had a whole new calendar.

46

The Vikings were the first Europeans to discover America. Half a millennium before Christopher Columbus "discovered" America, Viking chief Leif Eriksson of Greenland landed on the Island of Newfoundland in the year 1,000 AD. The Vikings under Leif Eriksson settled Newfoundland as well as discovering and settling Labrador further north in Canada.

47

Pope Gregory IX declared war on cats. He declared cats to be agents of devil worshippers. Not all cats, though; it was black moggies in particular. The Pope declared that they should be exterminated.

48

 Known worldwide for its four degrees lean, this freestanding bell tower was constructed in the 12th Century. When construction on the second story started, due to the unstable ground it was built on, the tower started to lean. After this, the lean only increased as the construction process went on, and it went on to become more iconic than the tower itself!

49

 This is because urine contains a very high ammonia content, and ammonia is one of the most powerful and readily available natural cleaners on this planet!

50

 At age 32, when he died, Alexander the Great had conquered and created the largest land-based empire the world has ever seen. It stretched from the Balkans to Pakistan. In 323 BC, Alexander fell ill, and after 12 days of excruciating pain, he seemingly passed away. However, his corpse didn't show any signs of rot or decomposition for a whole six days. Modern-day scientists believe Alexander suffered from the neurological disorder Guillain-Barré Syndrome. They believe that when he "died," he was actually just paralyzed and mentally aware. Basically, he was horrifically buried alive!

51

 They would lather their slaves in honey, which would serve a dual purpose of attracting any flies to their slaves rather than themselves, as well as trapping and killing the flies.

52

 Fought between Britain and Zanzibar and known as the Anglo-Zanzibar War, this war occurred on August 27, 1896. It was all over the ascension of the next Sultan in Zanzibar and resulted in a British victory.

53

During WWII, the British & Soviets launched a joint invasion of neutral Iran.

54

The UK government collected postcards as intelligence for the D-Day landings. Starting in 1942, the BBC issued a public appeal for postcards and photographs of mainland Europe's coast, from Norway to the Pyrenees. This was an intelligence-gathering exercise. Initiated by Lieutenant General Frederick Morgan, he was searching for the hardest beaches to defend. The postcards were sent to the War Office and helped form part of the decision to choose Normandy as the location for the eventual D-Day landings.

55

Cleopatra was the first member of her dynasty to speak Ancient Egyptian.

56

Count Dracula was inspired by a real person.

57

Spartan women owned most of the land and wealth in Sparta.

58

Only 6 people died in the Great Fire of London. The great fire of 1666 apparently traces its way to a baker's oven and caused massive damage across the city of London. However, despite destroying over 13,500 houses and displacing 80,000 people, it only claimed the lives of 6 unlucky Londoners.

59

The Ancient Egyptians used slabs of stone as pillows.

60

Adolf Hitler's nephew fought against the Nazis in World War II

61

Cleopatra wasn't Egyptian. She was part of the Ptolemy dynasty, who was derived from one of Alexander the Great's generals, Ptolemy.

62

The World War II army of the US is the biggest army in history. Due in part to the surge of wartime patriotism and in part because of conscription, the US Army numbered 12,000,000 soldiers by the end of the war in 1945. By 1943, the German military had reached 11,000,000 soldiers. By the end of the war, the Soviet Union's army (as formidable as it was) also reached 11 million soldiers.

63

The Soviet Union tried to snuff out the memory of Genghis Khan. During the Soviet-era rule of the late 20th century, simply mentioning the great conqueror's name was a crime against the USSR. The Soviets removed his story from school textbooks and outlawed pilgrimages to his birthplace of Khentii. After Mongolia gained its independence in the early 1990s, he was restored to his rightful place as a national hero of Mongolia. He appeared in the art and popular culture, as well as on Mongolian currency.

64

The first official Medals of Honor were awarded during the American Civil War.

65

In 1710, Native American leaders traveled to Britain to visit the Queen.

66 

During World War I, the French built a "fake Paris." Complete with a replica of Champs-Elysées and Gard Du Nord, this "fake Paris" was built by the French towards the end of WWI. It was built as a means of throwing off German bombers and fighter pilots flying over French skies. It also even had a fake railway that lit up at certain points to provide the illusion from above of a train moving along the tracks!

67

Spartans were so rich that nobody had to work.

68

One in 200 men are direct descendants of Genghis Khan. The Mongolian Emperor was known for siring many, many children – at least 11! Scientists conducted a study in 2003 that showed that one in 200 men share a Y chromosome with the conqueror. This may not sound like a lot, but you should consider that there are roughly 3.7 billion men on the planet. That makes a total of around 19 million men ancestors of the Great Khan!

69

Russia ran out of vodka when celebrating the end of World War II.

70

The Dutch-Scilly War lasted 335 years and had no battles or deaths.

Tsutomu Yamaguchi, a 29-year-old naval engineer, survived both atomic bombings in Hiroshima and Nagasaki. On August 6, 1945, he was less than 2 miles from the Hiroshima blast but survived and escaped the city. On August 9, after returning to his hometown Nagasaki, he endured the second atomic bombing with only minor injuries.

72

Before Julius Caesar invaded Britain, many Romans didn't believe it existed.

73

Alexander the Great named over 70 cities after himself.

74

It's believed that roughly 97% of history has been lost over time.

75

An ancient text called the Voynich Manuscript still baffles scientists. Hand-written in an unknown language, the Voynich Manuscript has been carbon-dated to roughly 1404 – 1438. Some of the pages are missing, and some of them are foldable pull-out pages, while most pages have illustrations. Hundreds of cryptographers and master codebreakers have tried to decipher it over the years, with none succeeding in grasping its meaning or origin.

76

Since the end of World War I, over 1,000 people have died from leftover unexploded bombs.

1

The ten highest mountain summits in the United States are all located in Alaska.

2

In Colorado, USA, there is still an active volcano. It last erupted about the same time as the pyramids were being built in Egypt.

3

Iceland does not have a railway system.

4

An estimated 50% of all gold ever mined on Earth came from a single plateau in South Africa: Witwatersrand.

5

The largest Japanese population outside of Japan stands at 1.6 million people who live in Brazil.

6

There are less than 30 ships in the Royal Canadian Navy which are less than most third-world countries.

7

There is an island called "Just Enough Room," where there's just enough room for a tree and a house.

8

For nearly 60 years, Texas didn't have an official state flag between 1879 & 1933. During that time, the Lone Star flag was active, but the unofficial flag.

9

Saint Lucia is the only country in the world named after a woman. The country was named after Saint Lucy of Syracuse by the French.

10

There is a town in Nebraska called Monowi with a population of one. The only resident is a woman who is the Mayor, Bartender, and Librarian.

11

Since 1955, 50% of the population of Niger is consistently under 16 years old. The total current population is 21,600,000.

12

Over 290 people have died climbing Mount Everest since 1922. Most deaths occur because of avalanches, and not all bodies have been recovered.

13

There are only two countries in the world that have the color purple in their flags: Nicaragua and Dominica.

14

Only 5% of the ocean has been explored.

15

The national animal of Scotland is a unicorn.

16

In Uganda, around 48% of the population is under 15 years of age.

17

There is a town in Indiana called Santa Claus.

18

San Marino is the fifth smallest country in the world (and the third smallest in Europe).

19

Houston is the most diverse city in the United States. As of 2010, 43.8% are Latino, 25.6% are White, 23.1% are Black, and 6% are Asian.

20

Disney World is actually larger than 17 other countries.

21

45 of the 50 most dangerous cities in the world (ranked by murder rate) are in America.

22

Australia has over 10,000 beaches. You could visit a new beach every day for over 27 years!

23

There is an uninhabited island in the Bahamas known as Pig Beach, which is populated entirely by swimming pigs.

24

On an island off the West Coast of Australia lies Lake Hillier, a bright bubble-gum pink lake, and scientists have yet to determine what causes its unique color.

25

Hawaii's state flag is the only US state flag to feature the Union Jack upon it.

26

The Dead Sea is one of the saltiest bodies of water in the world, with a salinity of around 30%, making it possible for people to float effortlessly.

27

Mount Everest's height is still increasing. The peak is rising by about 4 millimeters per year due to tectonic activity.

28

The Amazon Rainforest produces 20% of the world's oxygen and is often referred to as the "lungs of the Earth."

29

The Sahara Desert was once a lush, green area with lakes and rivers. Evidence of this is found in ancient cave paintings.

30

Antarctica contains about 60% of the world's fresh water, stored in its ice sheets.

31

The Great Wall of China is not a single continuous wall but a series of walls and fortifications built over several dynasties.

32

Mount Kilimanjaro in Tanzania is the highest peak in Africa and is unique for its three volcanic cones: Kibo, Mawenzi, and Shira.

33

Lake Baikal in Siberia is the world's deepest and oldest freshwater lake, reaching depths of over 1,600 meters (5,250 feet) and being around 25 million years old.

34

The Nile River, historically considered the longest river in the world, flows over 6,600 kilometers (4,100 miles) through northeastern Africa.

35

The Great Barrier Reef is the largest coral reef system in the world, stretching over 2,300 kilometers (1,430 miles).

36

Mount Fuji in Japan is an active stratovolcano and is considered a sacred symbol of Japan.

37

Lake Victoria is the largest lake in Africa by area and the second-largest freshwater lake in the world.

38

Iceland generates about 85% of its total energy supply from geothermal sources, thanks to its location on the Mid-Atlantic Ridge.

39

Moscow's metro system is renowned for its opulence and efficiency, with some stations designed like grand palaces.

40

Monaco is the second-smallest country in the world by area, covering just 2.02 square kilometers (0.78 square miles), but it has the highest population density.

41

The Atacama Desert in Chile is one of the driest places on Earth, with some weather stations having never recorded any rainfall.

42

Greenland's ice sheet is the second-largest in the world, covering about 80% of the island and contributing to rising sea levels.

43

Dubai is home to the Palm Islands, an artificial archipelago built using land reclamation techniques.

44

Mount Denali (formerly Mount McKinley) in Alaska is the highest peak in North America, standing at 6,190 meters (20,310 feet) above sea level.

45

The Gobi Desert, located in northern China and southern Mongolia, is known for its extreme temperature variations, ranging from scorching heat to frigid cold.

46

Lake Titicaca, located on the border of Peru and Bolivia, is the highest navigable lake in the world, situated at an altitude of about 3,812 meters (12,507 feet).

47

Yosemite Valley in California is famous for its stunning granite cliffs, waterfalls, and giant sequoia trees.

48

Borneo's rainforest is one of the oldest tropical rainforests in the world, estimated to be over 130 million years old.

49

Niagara Falls, straddling the border between Canada and the United States, consists of three major waterfalls: Horseshoe Falls, American Falls, and Bridal Veil Falls.

50

Japan is located on the Pacific Ring of Fire, a region known for its high seismic activity, including earthquakes and volcanoes.

51

Vatican City is the smallest independent state in the world, with an area of just 44 hectares (110 acres).

52

Lake Huron, one of the Great Lakes, is known for having the most shipwrecks of any of the Great Lakes, estimated at over 1,000.

53

Iceland's geothermal energy is so abundant that the country has even considered exporting this energy to other countries.

54

Nauru, a small island country in the Pacific, was once incredibly wealthy due to phosphate mining but is now one of the highest unemployment rates in the world.

55

The Danakil Depression in Ethiopia is one of the hottest places on Earth, with temperatures regularly exceeding 50°C (122°F).

56

The Great Salt Lake in Utah, USA, is the largest saltwater lake in the Western Hemisphere and is saltier than most oceanic waters.

57

Antarctica is the fifth-largest continent and is almost entirely covered by ice, with about 98% of its surface covered in ice sheets.

58

The Andes mountain range is the longest continental mountain range in the world, stretching over 7,000 kilometers (4,300 miles) along the western coast of South America.

59

Belize is home to the second-largest barrier reef in the world, the Mesoamerican Barrier Reef, which is a UNESCO World Heritage site.

60

Mount Etna, located on the east coast of Sicily, Italy, is one of the most active volcanoes in the world and has been erupting for over 500,000 years.

61

In addition to the Palm Islands, Dubai has also created The World Islands, an artificial archipelago that represents a map of the world.

62

Lake Eyre in Australia is the largest salt lake in Australia and can fill with water during rare and extreme rainfall events, but it is often dry.

63

Switzerland is famous for its policy of neutrality and has not been involved in a war since 1815.

64

Singapore has increased its land area by over 25% through land reclamation projects to accommodate its growing population.

65

Machu Picchu in Peru was rediscovered by American historian Hiram Bingham in 1911 and is one of the most well-preserved Incan ruins in the world.

66

The salinity of the Dead Sea is so high that people can float effortlessly on its surface without any swimming skills.

67

The faces of four U.S. presidents—George Washington, Thomas Jefferson, Theodore Roosevelt, and Abraham Lincoln—are carved into Mount Rushmore.

68

The Galápagos Islands, located in the Pacific Ocean, played a key role in Charles Darwin's development of the theory of evolution due to their unique biodiversity.

69

Greenland's ice cap is so large that it contains approximately 8% of the world's fresh water.

70

The Maldives is the lowest-lying country in the world, with its highest point reaching just 2.4 meters (7.9 feet) above sea level.

78 COOL FACTS OF SCIENCE PHYSICS TECHNOLOGY

1

The scientific term for brain freeze is "SPHENOPALATINE GANGLIONEURALGIA."

2

Car Remote Signal: If you point your car keys to your head, it increases the remote's signal range. The FLUIDS in your head act as a CONDUCTOR, allowing you to extend the remote's range by a few car lengths.

3

Soviet Russia needed lighthouses on their uninhabited Northern Coast, so they built AUTOMATED lighthouses powered by small NUCLEAR REACTORS.

4

When water freezes to ice cubes, it will take up 9% more VOLUME.

5

Before APPLE bought SIRI, it was originally going to be released as an app for ANDROID & BLACKBERRY.

6

The Speed of LIGHT Varies: Light travels slower in materials like water and can be slowed to a complete stop in certain conditions using BOSE-EINSTEIN condensates.

7

The first-ever VCR was the size of a piano. When the first VCR (Video Camera Recorder) was made in 1956, it was the size of a piano. Way bigger than I would have guessed!

8

First Computer Bug: The term "computer bug" originated when a real moth was found causing issues inside the HARVARD MARK II computer in 1947.

9

A PETABYTE is a lot of data. We all know 1 GB is the same as 1024 MB, but did you know that 1 petabyte (PB) is equivalent to 1024 terabytes (TB)? To give an example of how big this is, a 1 PB hard drive could hold 13.3 years of HD-TV VIDEO. A 50 PB hard drive could hold the entire written works of mankind, from the beginning of recorded history, in all languages.

ALEXA is always listening to your conversations. This probably isn't new to you. Siri has been doing it **FOREVER**. Alexa **STORES** your dialogue history in its CLOUD to help improve your Alexa experience. But you can review and delete these recordings, either in bulk or individually.

Quantum Computing Power: A quantum computer can solve complex problems in **SECONDS** that would take a traditional supercomputer thousands of years to complete.

There are **AMISH** computers. There are computers specially designed **WITHOUT** internet, video, or music capabilities, just for the Amish. The features include word processing, drawing, accounting, spreadsheets, and more – but **NOT** much more.

3D Printing Organs: 3D printing technology is advancing to the point where HUMAN organs, like kidneys and hearts, are being printed layer by layer for potential use in TRANSPLANTS

AI's Chess Mastery: In 1997, IBM'S DEEP BLUE became the first computer to DEFEAT a reigning world chess champion, Garry Kasparov, in a match.

The FIRST ONLINE GAMING was before the year 2000. SEGA DREAMCAST was the first 128-BIT console to hit the market. Released in 1999, it was the first console that allowed REAL-TIME ONLINE PLAY. Unfortunately, it was a little too early for its time, as back then, most internet connections were not reliable enough.

The first product SCANNED was a packet of chewing gum in 1974. Known as the Universal Product Code (UPC), a system that is still used today.

97% of people use GOOGLE as a SPELLCHECKER. Most everyone, anyway! I know I'm definitely among that 97%!

19

DNA Data Storage: Scientists have developed techniques to store data in DNA, with one gram of DNA theoretically capable of holding **215 PETABYTES** (215 million gigabytes) of data.

20

GOOGLE SEARCHES hit the **BILLIONS** every month.

21

Self-Driving Cars: The first autonomous vehicle prototype was created by Carnegie Mellon University's Navlab project in the 1980s, paving the way for today's self-driving cars.

22

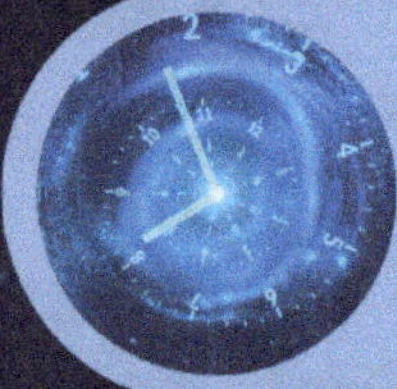

In 2009, Stephen Hawking held a reception for **TIME TRAVELERS** but didn't publicize it until after. This way, only those who could time travel would be able to attend.

23

"Phantom Vibration Syndrome" is the name for when someone thinks their phone is vibrating, but it **ISN'T**.

24

Smoking will void your **APPLE WARRANTY**.

25

TECHNOLOGY is now influencing **BABY NAMES**. In 2012, at least six girls were named **APPLE**, 49 boys were named **MAC**, and at least 17 girls were named **SIRI**. However, the number of babies named **ALEXA** in the U.S. has dropped from 6,050 in 2015 (the year Amazon's Alexa became available) to 3,053 in 2018. Alexa was the 32nd most popular name for girls born in 2015 but dropped to 90th place in 2018.

26

BLIND people can use **CELL PHONES**. There is special **BRAILLE** technology and accessories for blind people to use cell phones. It uses special **PINS** that go up and down so the user can touch and read the info.

27

The **FIRST** cell phone **CALL** was in New York City.

28

The first **COMMERCIAL TEXT MESSAGE** was sent in 1992.

29

Over 6,000 new **COMPUTER VIRUSSES** are created and released every month. This number has drastically risen since 1990 Today, 90% of emails contain some form of malware, and most people **DON'T** know about it.

30

iPHONES were almost in the shape of an **APPLE**. The original design for an iPhone was in the shape of a literal apple. It was initially designed as a flip phone with a push keypad. When closed, it looked like the Apple logo.

31

NASA's internet speed is **91 GB** per second.

32

NOKIA is the largest company from **FINLAND**.

33

Although **GPS** is free for the world to use, it costs **$2 MILLION** per day to operate, funded by American tax revenue.

34

More people have **CELL PHONES** than **TOILETS**.

35

Using a **THINNER FONT** can **SAVE** printer ink.

36

Higgs Boson Discovery: The elusive Higgs boson particle, essential for understanding why particles have mass, was discovered in 2012 at the Large Hadron Collider, confirming a key aspect of the Standard Model of particle physics.

37

Moore's Law: Gordon Moore, co-founder of Intel, predicted in 1965 that the number of transistors on a microchip would double approximately every two years, driving exponential growth in computing power. This prediction has largely held true for several decades.

38

Some people are AFRAID of TECHNOLOGY. Let's just hope this phobia doesn't stop them from reading these technology facts!

39

The MOST EXPENSIVE phone number cost millions. Back in 2006, Qatar Telecom hosted a charity auction where they sold the phone number 666-6666. It sold for $2.75 million, bought by an anonymous bidder.

40

There's a term for old people who use the internet – SILVER SURFERS

41

Smartphone Computing Power: Modern smartphones have more computing power than the computers used to land astronauts on the Moon during the Apollo missions.

42

Finding a **SECURITY BUG** in Facebook's code will pay off. To be exact, Facebook pays **$500** for reporting any vulnerability in its security. Even better, $500 is just the minimum that it starts at.

43

CRISPR Revolution: CRISPR-Cas9 is a revolutionary gene-editing technology that allows for precise modifications to DNA, holding potential for treating genetic disorders and transforming biotechnology.

44

If you heat up a magnet, it will lose its magnetism.

45

The **PASSWORDS** for the nuclear missiles were just a string of ZEROS.

46

The **QWERTY keyboard** was originally designed to slow you down. When typewriters were introduced, typing too fast would jam the keys. Using a QWERTY keyboard spaced out commonly used characters to slow typists down and prevent jamming.

47

The **FIRST** webpage is still running. In 1991, Tim Berners-Lee was working on developing the **World Wide Web**. There are no graphics and no background, just plain text and links on how to use the internet!

48

Over **90%** of the world's currency is **DIGITAL**

49

Tech companies often **TEST** their products in **NEW ZEALAND**. It is such a diverse country with English-speaking residents, which makes it a **GREAT** place for testing. But the main reason is that since it's somewhat isolated, news about a product **FAILING** won't spread very fast.

50

Graphene, a one-atom-thick sheet of carbon atoms arranged in a hexagonal lattice, is the strongest material ever tested, 200 times stronger than steel yet incredibly lightweight.

51

An average 21-year-old has spent 5,000 hours playing video games.

52

Most of today's successful companies started in GARAGES. That's right, aside from just Apple, other huge name companies, such as HP, Google, and Microsoft

53

DNA stores information far more efficiently than current digital devices. One gram of DNA can hold approximately 215 million gigabytes of data.

54

Most internet traffic isn't from real humans. About 51% of internet traffic is non-human. Over 30% is from hacking programs, spammers, and phishing. Be careful with your computer security!

55

CAPTCHA is a long acronym. It stands for "Completely Automatic Public Turning Test to Tell Computers and Humans Apart." Even though some artificial intelligence can get through CATCHPA, it's still useful in blocking some bots.

Most **INTERNET** traffic **ISN'T** from real humans. About **51%** of internet traffic is non-human. Over 30% is from **HACKING** programs, spammers, and phishing. Be careful with your computer security!

There **WASN'T** an app store on the **FIRST** iPhone.

There is a machine that can predict heart attacks. Researchers "trained" a machine-learning algorithm that was able to predict heart attacks. It can predict heart attacks up to four hours before they happened – with 80% accuracy.

DIGITAL tech is **GOOD** for the environment. It is estimated that digital technology could **REDUCE** global carbon emissions by **20%** by 2030.

LASERS are not only used for precision cutting or measuring but are also used to **COMMUNICATE** with **SPACECRAFTS** millions of kilometers away from Earth.

Robot laws are being put into place

62

DIGITAL music sales SURPASSED physical sales in 2014. Since MP3 players arrived, digital music sales have been slowly rising. Once SPOTIFY came out in 2008, it seemed the age of physical music was over. In 2014, download sales and subscriptions made $6.85 billion, while physical sales were just barely under it at $6.82 billion.

63

We only keep 1 out of every 10 apps we try.

64

The THREE most common PASSWORDS are also the WEAKEST. The top three most used passwords are 123456, password, and 12345. Definitely don't use any of those next time you need a password change!

65

Einstein's theory of relativity predicts that time moves slower in places with stronger gravity, an effect known as gravitational time dilation.

66

Dark matter makes up about 27% of the universe, while ordinary matter accounts for only about 5%. The rest is dark energy.

There is also AI that can PREDICT epidemics. An AI was created (with 87% ACCUCRACY) to determine disease outbreaks, such as dengue fever. There are hopes to use this tech to predict outbreaks of more serious diseases like Ebola and Zika.

GOOGLE uses the same amount of ENERGY as 200,000 homes. It's no surprise this tech powerhouse NEEDS A LOT OF power! That accounts for about 0.013% of the entire world's energy use. And while not all of their energy is from wind and solar, they purchase carbon offsets which leaves them with no carbon footprint!

Most of the purchases in China are done with mobile phones.

Millions of tons of technology are thrown out each year. Specifically, 220 million tons of old computers, along with other devices, are thrown away every year in the U.S. alone.

There is now technology BUILT into some GUNS in America that allow a gun's owner to CONTROL the SAFETY-CATCH using their SMARTPHONE or TABLET.

The world's largest particle accelerator, the Large Hadron Collider (LHC), has a circumference of 27 kilometers and is built on the border between France and Switzerland.

The Hubble Space Telescope can see objects located up to 13.4 billion light-years away, allowing us to look back in time almost to the beginning of the universe.

74

Quantum entanglement is a phenomenon where particles become linked, and the state of one instantaneously influences the state of another, even if they are light-years apart.

75

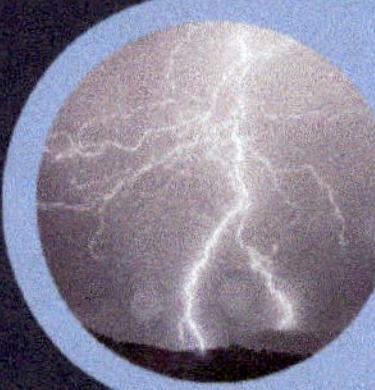

Lightning Temperature: A bolt of lightning can reach **53,540** degrees Fahrenheit, which is **five times hotter** than the surface of the sun.

Walmart uses big data to understand customer behavior. They discovered that strawberry Pop-Tarts and beer are the most purchased items before a hurricane.

The average cumulus cloud weighs about 1.1 million pounds. This is due to the vast amount of water droplets condensed within the cloud.

Filipinos use social media more than Americans. Among adult users in the Philippines, 93% use social networking sites, which is quite higher than the 74% that use it in the U.S.

77 HUMAN'S FACTS

1. Researchers have found that FLOSSING your teeth can HELP your MEMORY. Flossing prevents gum disease, which prevents stiff blood vessels, which cause memory issues.

2. Standing around BURNS calories. On average, a 150-pound person burns 114 calories per hour while standing and doing nothing.

3. BANGING your head against a wall for one hour burns 150 calories. If you're not keen on losing brain cells, you might want to skip this calorie-burning idea! A much SAFER way to burn 150 calories is to TAKE YOUR DOG for a 45-minute walk.

4. During your lifetime, you will produce enough SALIVA to fill 50 bathtubs! The average person produces roughly one ounce (30 ml) of saliva every hour. That's an average of 69 gallons (263 liters) per year.

5. Our hearts PUMP 2000 gallons of blood each day.

6. The human eye is so SENSITIVE that if the Earth were flat and it was a dark night, a candle's flame could be seen from 30 miles away.

7. Most Korean people DON'T have ARMPIT ODOR. Research found that only 0.006% of the Korean population has the ABCC11 gene, which causes armpit odor.

8. Human blood cells have DIFFERENT lifespans. RED blood cells circulate for about four months, while WHITE blood cells range from a few hours to several days.

9. The human body has enough carbon to fill 1000 pencils.

10. In 30 minutes, the human body gives off enough HEAT to bring a gallon of water to the boil.

11. HICCUPS can last a very long time. The record is held by Charles Osborne, who had hiccups for 68 years.

12. People burn MORE calories being asleep THAN they do by watching TV.

13. In your mouth alone, there are MORE bacteria THAN people in the entire world.

14. The human brain accounts for approximately 20% of the body's total energy consumption, even though it only makes up about 2% of the body's weight.

15. Yawning actually WAKES you UP. Yawning gets more air into the lungs, thus increasing OXYGEN to the brain.

16. Frequent jet lag can DAMAGE memory. Stress hormones released during jet lag can damage the temporal lobe and memory.

17. EXCESSIVE stress has been shown to ALTER brain cells, brain structure, and brain function.

18. While flying in an airplane, your hair will grow at TWICE the rate it usually does.

19. Every 3-4 seconds, around 50,000 cells in your body will DIE and be replaced by new ones.

20. The chances of living to be 100 years old are VERY slim for most people, and only one out of every two billion people will live to be 116 years old.

21. A vibrant social life is crucial for mental and physical well-being. Social interactions are linked to better health outcomes and increased life satisfaction.

22. Studies have shown that laughter increases the production of antibodies and activates immune cells, which helps to improve your body's defense mechanisms against illnesses.

23. Studies have shown that chewing gum can improve memory, enhance cognitive performance, and even help you stay focused longer.

24. The tongue is the ONLY muscle in one's body that is attached from one end.

25. The distance from your wrist to your elbow is the SAME length as your foot.

26 The SMALLEST bone in your body is in your ear. Known as the *stapes bone*, it is vital in transferring vibrations from sounds into the inner ear.

27 Every 10 years, the human skeleton REPAIRS and RENEWS itself.

28 Bones are FOUR times STRONGER than concrete.

29 Your nose can DIFFERENTIATE between a WIDE RANGE OF different odors.

30 More than half of the bones in the human body are found in our HANDS and FEET.

31 The weight of the brain is about 1.36 kg.

32 Your fingerprints aren't the only part of your body that are completely unique to you. Your TONGUE also has a unique pattern and print.

33 If you're a man, the SMALLEST cells in your body are SPERM CELLS.

34 If you're a female, your heart beats QUICKER than your male counterparts.

35 No matter how many times you try, it's IMPOSSIBLE to sneeze and keep your eyes open at the same time.

36 The human brain is so powerful that it can distinguish between background noise and the voice on the phone in noisy rooms.

37 About 10% of the world's population is LEFT-HANDED, and studies suggest that people on the autism spectrum may have a HIGHER likelihood of being left-handed compared to the general population.

38 Humans share about 98.8% of their DNA with chimpanzees, and around 60% with fruit flies.

39 The human brain contains around 86 billion neurons, each connected to thousands of other neurons, forming an intricate network responsible for all thoughts, memories, and actions.

40 The human brain is the FATTEST organ in the body and may consist of at least 60% fat.

41 The average human body carries about 5 pounds (2.3 kg) of bacteria, which play a crucial role in digestion, immune function, and even mental health. These microorganisms are so vital that they're often referred to as a "second genome," influencing various aspects of health.

42 There are 45 miles of nerves in the human body.

43 INTELLIGENT people often avoid POINTLESS arguments by remaining silent when annoyed. This behavior is linked to higher levels of self-control and emotional regulation.

44 Posting fitness routines on social media can be associated with a range of PSYCHOLOGICAL issues. Research suggests that such behavior might be linked to UNDERLYING insecurities or a need for validation.

45 CHEROPHOBIA is the irrational fear of happiness. Individuals with this phobia often AVOID situations perceived as fun or joyful due to an underlying fear that these moments will lead to negative consequences.

46 MEN typically grow BORED of shopping after about 26 minutes, whereas women can shop for around 2 hours before feeling tired. This difference is influenced by varying interests and shopping goals.

47 95% of people text things they wouldn't say in person. This tendency highlights the difference between online and face-to-face communication dynamics.

48 People are more likely to RETURN a lost wallet if it contains a picture of A CHILD. This is because PERSONAL photos elicit a sense of empathy and responsibility.

49 70% of people prefer OLD songs due to the EMOTIONAL memories they evoke. NOSTALGIA plays a significant role in why we enjoy certain music.

50 We tend to automatically trust and agree with people we like and are attracted to. This phenomenon is known as the HALO EFFECT, where positive feelings toward someone influence our judgments of them.

51 The way people TREAT their EMPLOYEES often reflects their own CHARACTER. Respectful treatment of others is indicative of a person's integrity and values.

52 Negative information is often more memorable than positive information. This tendency, known as negativity bias, is thought to be an evolutionary adaptation for survival.

53 Bilingual individuals may experience shifts in personality depending on the language they are speaking. This phenomenon can reflect different cultural norms and cognitive styles associated with each language.

54 Creative abilities can be HEIGHTENED during nighttime. The relaxed state of the brain during late hours can foster creative thinking and problem-solving.

55 People often BLAME others for their own mistakes. This behavior, known as the actor-observer effect, helps protect self-esteem and manage cognitive dissonance.

56 You will be HAPPIER when doing things that scare you. This is based on psychology, specifically the concept of overcoming fears and the sense of accomplishment.

57 97% of people write their names when given a new pen. This habit reflects the tendency to MARK ownership and IDENTIFY in personal items.

58 Those who give the most advice often have their own unresolved issues. This is sometimes referred to as the "advice-giving paradox," where individuals project their own problems onto others.

59 People who speak quickly and infrequently may be MORE likely to KEEP secrets. This communication style can be associated with higher levels of privacy and reserve.

60 The first teardrop from the RIGHT eye during crying is typically associated with HAPPINESS. This can be linked to the emotional significance and context of the tears.

61 Memory recall is often IMPAIRED during the first few seconds after waking up. This temporary amnesia is due to the brain transitioning from sleep to wakefulness.

62 Parents who view failure as a learning opportunity help their children DEVELOP a growth mindset. This approach encourages the belief that intelligence and abilities can be developed through effort.

63 People are more likely to CONFESS to things when they are physically TIRED. Fatigue REDUCES self-control and can make individuals more honest.

64 Déjà vu often involves recalling a previous conversation or dream. This phenomenon occurs when the brain experiences a sense of familiarity without a clear source.

65 Initial information often has a disproportionate influence on future decisions. This is known as the anchoring effect, where early information serves as a reference point.

66 Judgments about things are often influenced by how they make us feel rather than their objective value. This is related to affective forecasting, where emotions shape perceptions.

67 The way you hold your fist can REVEAL aspects of your PERNONALITY. For example, a tightly clenched fist may signify tension or defensiveness.

68 People tend to remember the FIRST and LAST items in a list better than those in the middle. This is known as the serial position effect.

69 The color RED can increase attractiveness and convey signals of health and status. Red triggers primal responses related to sexuality and dominance.

70 Excessive NODDING during a conversation may indicate a LOSS of interest. While nodding is often a sign of agreement, OVERUSE can signal disinterest while attempting to appear polite.

71 Human behavior can be CONTAGIOUS due to mirror neurons. These neurons help us mimic and empathize with the actions of others.

72 Observing gestures can provide insights into agreement or disagreement. Non-verbal cues often reveal more about a person's true feelings than their words.

73 *Food Craving Effect:* Research shows that when you're hungry, you're not only more likely to buy more food but also tend to purchase more non-food items. This explains why you might buy more when shopping on an empty stomach.

74 *Framing Effect:* The way information is presented can significantly influence people's decisions, even if the content remains unchanged. For example, a food item described as "90% fat-free" is often perceived as better than the same item labeled "contains 10% fat." This effect is widely used in marketing and advertising to steer customer choices in a favorable direction.

75 *Bad Apple Effect:* The presence of one negative person in a group can reduce the performance and morale of the entire group. This happens because negative behaviors can spread and influence the attitudes and actions of others.

76 *Traffic Light Effect:* At intersections with traffic lights, people are more likely to run a red light if they see other cars doing the same, even though they know it's dangerous. This highlights the strong influence of social behavior on individual decisions in everyday situations.

77 *Scarcity Effect:* When something becomes scarce or appears to be running out, people tend to value it more highly and are willing to pay more for it. This is why "one-day-only" sales or "limited stock" promotions are so effective in driving sales.

1

Gold doesn't tarnish or rust because it doesn't react easily with most chemicals.

2

Caffeine in coffee acts as a natural pesticide for coffee plants

3

Fresh-cut grass releases a chemical called 'green leaf volatiles' when damaged.

4

Different chemicals give fireworks their colors; for example, strontium makes red, and copper makes blue.

5

Helium's Voice Effect: Inhaling helium makes your voice sound high-pitched because sound travels faster in helium than in air.

6

Carbon dioxide (CO_2) is what makes soft drinks fizzy.

7

Mixing baking soda (sodium bicarbonate) with vinegar (acetic acid) produces carbon dioxide gas, making bubbles.

8

Mercury is the only metal that is liquid at room temperature due to its weak atomic bonding.

9

Water has one of the highest heat capacities of any substance, which is why it takes a long time to heat up or cool down.

10

Silicon is a chemical element used in electronics, while silicone is a synthetic polymer used in everything from cookware to medical implants.

11

Dry ice is solid carbon dioxide (CO_2) and sublimates directly from a solid to a gas without passing through a liquid phase.

12

Chlorine is used in pools because it's an effective disinfectant, killing bacteria and other pathogens.

13

Sulfur compounds, particularly hydrogen sulfide, are responsible for the smell of rotten eggs.

14

Carbon exists in several forms, including graphite, diamond, and graphene, each with distinct physical properties.

15

Ethanol is commonly used in hand sanitizers because it effectively kills a wide range of microbes.

16

Lemon juice is acidic, and soap is basic.

17

Liquid nitrogen is so cold that it boils at -196°C (-321°F).

18

Fluorine is the most reactive and electronegative of all elements, readily forming compounds with almost all other elements.

19

Human blood has a pH of about 7.4, making it slightly basic (alkaline).

20

Nitrogen is a key component of fertilizers, essential for plant growth.

21

Bromine is one of only two elements (the other being mercury) that is liquid at room temperature.

22

Methane is a potent greenhouse gas, about 25 times more effective at trapping heat in the atmosphere than carbon dioxide over a 100-year period.

23

Glycerol, also known as glycerin, is a humectant that attracts moisture to the skin, making it a common ingredient in lotions and creams.

24

Sulfuric acid is one of the most produced and used chemicals in the world, essential for manufacturing fertilizers, chemicals, and in petroleum refining.

25

Caffeine is a naturally occurring stimulant found in coffee, tea, and chocolate, chemically classified as an alkaloid.

26

Ice floats on water because it is less dense than liquid water.

27

Hydrogen is the lightest and most abundant element in the universe.

28

Copper turns green over time because it reacts with air to form a green patina.

29

Vitamin C, or ascorbic acid, is important for your body's immune system.

30

The smell of gasoline comes from a chemical called benzene.

31

Hot packs contain chemicals that release heat when mixed, and cold packs contain chemicals that absorb heat.

32

Tomatoes are red because they contain a pigment called lycopene.

33

Cinnamon's smell comes from a chemical called cinnamaldehyde.

34

Glow sticks light up when you crack them because two chemicals mix and react to produce light.

35

Talc is the softest mineral on the Mohs hardness scale, which is why it's used in baby powder.

36

Milk turns sour when bacteria produce lactic acid, which lowers the pH.

37

Ammonia has a strong, sharp smell and is often used in cleaning products.

38

Flamingos are pink because of the pigments in the algae and shrimp they eat.

A skunk's smell comes from sulfur-containing chemicals called thiols.

Silver tarnishes when it reacts with sulfur in the air to form silver sulfide, which is black.

Carrots are orange because they contain beta-carotene, which the body converts to vitamin A.

Noble gases like helium, neon, and argon don't react with other elements because they have a full outer electron shell.

Diamonds are the hardest natural material on Earth because of how their carbon atoms are arranged.

Epsom salt is made of magnesium sulfate and is used in baths to soothe sore muscles.

Pineapple contains an enzyme called bromelain that breaks down proteins, which is why it can tenderize meat.

46

Mint feels cold because it contains menthol, which activates the same nerves as cold temperatures.

47

Bread goes stale because the starch in it crystallizes over time.

48

Mixing lemon juice with baking soda causes a reaction that produces carbon dioxide bubbles.

49

Highlighters glow under UV light because they contain fluorescent dyes.

50

When salt is added to ice, it lowers the freezing point, which is why it's used to melt ice on roads.

51

Soaking an egg in vinegar dissolves the shell because vinegar is an acid that reacts with calcium carbonate.

52

Pop Rocks candy pops in your mouth because it contains pressurized carbon dioxide gas.

53

The periodic table we use today has 118 confirmed elements, but new elements could still be discovered or created in the lab.

54

Glass is often called a supercooled liquid because it lacks a crystal structure, although it behaves like a solid.

55

Oxygen is colorless as a gas but is pale blue as a liquid. It's also the most abundant element in the Earth's crust.

56

White phosphorus glows in the dark when exposed to oxygen, a phenomenon known as chemiluminescence.

57

Stainless steel doesn't rust because it contains chromium, which forms a protective layer of chromium oxide.

58

The hydrochloric acid in your stomach is strong enough to dissolve metal, yet your stomach lining is protected by a thick layer of mucus.

59

The human body is made up of 60 different elements, with oxygen, carbon, hydrogen, and nitrogen making up 96% of the body's mass.

60

Chlorophyll, the green pigment in plants, is structurally similar to hemoglobin in human blood, except it contains magnesium instead of iron.

61

The saltiness of the ocean comes from minerals washed out of rocks on land, primarily sodium chloride.

62

Milk of Magnesia, used as an antacid, contains magnesium hydroxide, which neutralizes stomach acid.

63

Fluoride in toothpaste helps prevent cavities by strengthening tooth enamel.

64

Alkali metals like sodium and potassium are so reactive that they can explode when they come into contact with water.

65

Heavy water (D_2O) contains deuterium, a heavier isotope of hydrogen, and is used in nuclear reactors as a neutron moderator.

66

Plastics, nylon, and even DNA are made of polymers, long chains of repeating units that give these materials their unique properties.

When metal salts are added to a solution of sodium silicate, they form a "chemical garden," where colorful, plant-like structures grow.

Some metals, like nitinol, can "remember" their shape. When bent, they return to their original form when heated, a property used in various medical devices.

Caffeine works by blocking adenosine receptors in your brain, making you feel more awake.

Lemon juice can be used as invisible ink; it turns brown when heated to reveal hidden messages.

Carbon-14 dating is used to determine the age of ancient objects up to about 50,000 years old.

Aspirin was originally derived from willow bark, which contains salicin, a natural pain reliever.

Sulfur is a key component in gunpowder, which is used in fireworks to create explosions.

74

Bananas contain potassium, and a small fraction of it is the radioactive isotope potassium-40. Eating one banana exposes you to a tiny amount of radiation.

75

Many elements produce characteristic colors when burned; for instance, lithium gives a red flame, sodium gives yellow, and copper gives blue or green.

76

For every particle of matter, there is an antiparticle with the same mass but opposite charge. When matter and antimatter meet, they annihilate each other.

1

If a Polar Bear and a Grizzly Bear mate, their offspring is called a "Pizzly Bear."

2

The scientific name for the Giant Anteater is Myrmecophaga Tridactyla. This means "ant eating with three fingers."

3

At birth, a baby panda is smaller than a mouse.

4

The Bagheera kiplingi spider was discovered in the 1800s and is the only species of spider that has been classified as vegetarian.

5

Octopuses and squids have beaks. The beak is made of keratin – the same material that a bird's beak and our fingernails are made of.

6

Those cute furry bits inside a cat's ear are called "ear furnishings." They ensure that dirt doesn't go inside and also helps them to hear well.

7

The color red doesn't really make bulls angry; they are partially color-blind.

8

When mice live in the wild, they typically only live for about six months. This is mostly due to the fact that they're a good source of food for other animals. However, in a controlled environment, like being kept as a pet, they can live up to two years.

9

A wildlife technician, Richard Thomas, took the famous tongue-twister "How much wood would a woodchuck chuck if a woodchuck could chuck wood" and calculated a rough estimate of what the answer would actually be. It came out to be around 700 pounds.

10

Scientists discovered sharks living in an active underwater volcano. Divers cannot investigate because they would get burns from the acidity and heat.

11

Llamas can be used as guards against coyote attacks on sheep herds. Studies have proven that just one guard llama is an effective protector and can even kill the attacking coyotes.

12

Many animals are able to predict earthquakes to varying levels of success. Yet, snakes are the most reliable, sensing earthquakes from as far as 75 miles away (121 km). They can even sense an earthquake five days before it actually occurs! When snakes sense an earthquake, they often leave their nests, even if the temperature is too cold.

13

If you lift a kangaroo's tail off the ground, it can't hop. Kangaroos use their tails for balance while hopping. If you elevate their tail, they will lose balance and fall over. There are cases where kangaroos have lost their tails and can still move around. But it took them a long time to adjust, and they can only move small distances at a time!

14

Birds are the closest living relatives of crocodilians, as well as the descendants of extinct dinosaurs with feathers. This makes them the only surviving dinosaurs.

15

Small as they may be, ladybugs have a unique smell that humans are incredibly sensitive to.

16

Polar bears could eat as many as 10 penguins in a single sitting...If they didn't live at opposite ends of the earth! With an average weight of 500 pounds (227 kg) and consuming approximately 20% of their weight per meal, polar bears can devour around 100 pounds of food at once

17

There is a species of spider called the Hobo Spider. The hobo spider (Eratigena agrestis) can be found in various places around the world, including Europe, Central Asia, and parts of western North America. This crafty little critter doesn't live in a standard spider web. Instead, it constructs a funnel made of web in the ground and waits for its prey to stumble into it.

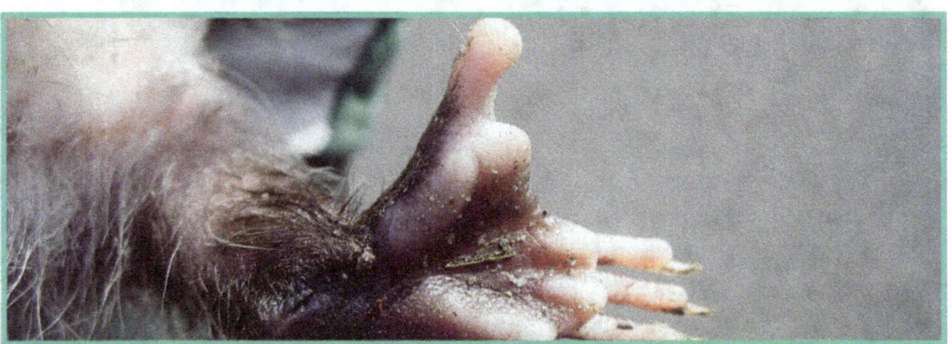

18

Only primates, humans, and opossums have opposable thumbs. Out of these, the opossum is the only one with no thumbnail.

19

It's not just humans who are right or left-handed. Most female cats prefer using their right paw, and males are more likely to be left-pawed.

Honeybees can recognize human faces. For a long time, we believed that only large-brained mammals could distinguish faces. But the humble honeybee shook that theory up! Bees can distinguish between many different flowers, so it was theorized that they might tell people apart. Scientists discovered that honeybees could recognize a familiar face, even days after being trained to do so. Fun Fact: Bees see faces in a compilation of 5,000 individual images – kind of like pixels.

A lion's roar can be heard from 5 miles away.

A baby octopus is about the size of a flea when it is born.

A crocodile can't poke its tongue out.

Octopuses only touch in situations of mating or aggression. Female octopuses sometimes do both, strangling and eating the male after mating.

Not all hamsters are small. Although some hamsters are as small as 2-4 inches, the largest ones are approximately 13 inches long.

26

A swarm of 20,000 bees followed a car for two days as their queen was trapped inside. A 68-year-old grandmother returning from a nature reserve was shocked to find her car covered in bees after the queen bee got stuck. The bees were safely removed, and the lovely old lady made her way home. However, much to her surprise, the bees were back the next day! It seems that the queen bee was still stuck inside, and the bees followed her the whole way home. This time, they were all removed, and they, fortunately, didn't return!

27

Sea otters hold hands when they sleep so they don't drift away from each other.

28

Squirrels cause approximately 10-20% of US power outages.

29

A small child could swim through the veins of a blue whale.

30

A group of parrots is known as a pandemonium of parrots.

31

In Switzerland, it is illegal to own just one guinea pig. This is because guinea pigs are social animals, and they are considered victims of abuse if they are alone.

32

Sharks have been around for over 400 million years and have survived five major planet extinctions. That makes them older than humanity and even the legendary dinosaurs.

Giraffes are 30 times more likely to get hit by lightning than people. True, there are only five well-documented fatal lightning strikes on giraffes between 1996 and 2010. But due to the population of the species being just 140,000 during this time, it makes for about 0.003 lightning deaths per thousand giraffes each year. This is 30 times the equivalent fatality rate for humans.

Chimpanzees don't normally attack to kill. Instead, they aim for the face, fingers, and genitals and will leave the opponent alive.

A cat can balance ten dice on its paw.

Cats can hear ultrasound.

When male bees mate, their testicles explode. This leaves the tip of their genitals inside the queen and is a way to stop another male bee from mating with the queen.

38

Herring fish communicate by using flatulence.

39

A study has shown that a male zebra finch is less likely to court a female zebra finch if he did not form any social friendships with female zebra finches when younger.

40

Animals yawn based on how large their brain is. The bigger the brain, the longer they will yawn.

41

If you keep a goldfish in a dark room, it will become pale.

42

Cockroaches can live for up to nine days without their heads.

43

The largest piece of fossilised dinosaur poo discovered is over 30cm long and over two litres in volume. Believed to be a Tyrannosaurus rex turd, the fossilised dung (also named a 'coprolite') is helping scientists better understand what the dinosaur ate.

44 Animals can experience time differently from humans. To smaller animals, the world around them moves more slowly compared to humans. Salamanders and lizards, for example, experience time more slowly than cats and dogs. This is because the perception of time depends on how quickly the brain can process incoming information.

45 Dogs can pick up diseases like cancer and diabetes in humans before the onset of visible symptoms.

46 The cute golden poison dart frog contains enough poison to kill up to 20 adults.

47 Zebras have only one toe on each foot.

48 Dinosaurs would swallow large rocks which stayed in their stomach to help churn and digest food.

49 The world's oldest dog lived to 29.5 years old. While the median age a dog reaches tends to be about 10-15 years, one Australian cattle dog, 'Bluey', survived to the ripe old age of 29.5.

50 A honey badger's skin is so thick, they can withstand multiple machete strikes, arrows and spears.

51 Dogs sweat through their foot pads to help keep them cool. They also keep cool by panting.

52

Colombian drug lord Pablo Escobar kept four Hippos in his estate before his death in 1993. Deemed too much hassle to move by authorities, his Hippos were left there and have since bred and escaped becoming an invasive species of Colombia.

53

Ants don't have lungs. They instead breathe through spiracles, nine or ten tiny openings, depending on the species.

54

The world's biggest-ever recorded turtle was a Leatherback Turtle that washed up in Harlech Beach, Wales, in 1988.

55

Octopuses have three hearts: two pump blood to the gills, while the third pumps it to the rest of the body. When an octopus swims, the heart that pumps blood to the body actually stops beating, which is why octopuses prefer crawling to conserve energy.

56

In 2013, wild boars were found roaming Ireland, thought to have been re-introduced illegally by poachers.

57 The bumblebee bat is not only the world's smallest bat, but it is also the world's smallest mammal.

58 A Dachshund (a.k.a. a sausage dog) was originally bred to hunt in low, narrow badger burrows.

59 A scorpion can hold its breath for 1 week.

60 Slugs have 4 noses.

61 Only female mosquitoes bite.

62 As part of the initiative to clean up the Ganges River of human corpses in the 1990s, the Indian government trained snapping turtles to eat human remains.

63 Dogs and cats can detect negative energy. These pets can see ghosts too.

64 Dogs like squeaky toys because the sound mimics that of captured prey.

65 The world's oldest cat lived to 38 years and three days old. Creme Puff was the oldest cat to ever live.

66 The American Veterinary Dental Society states that 80% of Dogs and 70% of cats show signs of oral disease by age 3.

67

Wolves have about 200 million scent cells. Humans have only about 5 million.

68

Cat whiskers are so sensitive they can detect the slightest change in air current.

69

Crocodiles have an average life span of 70 to 100 years.

70

Cats spend nearly 1/3 of their waking hours cleaning themselves.

71

Vampire bats are the only mammals in the world that live entirely on blood.

72

A butterfly sees you through their 12,000 eyes

73

Dogs have 28 baby teeth and 42 permanent teeth.

74

36 human hearts could fit inside a giraffe's heart.

75

Chocolate can kill dogs; it directly affects their heart and nervous system.

76

When baby monkeys are born they grab their mother's legs and pull themselves out.

77

Cows have best friends and can become stressed when separated from them.

78 Cats have 26 baby teeth and 30 permanent teeth.

79 Cats have 32 muscles in each ear.

80 Polar bear skin is black!

81 Starfish do not have a brain.

82 Fleas can jump 350 times its body length.

83 The only mammal capable of flight is the bat.

85 Hummingbirds are the only birds that can fly backwards.

84 A newborn kangaroo is the size of a lima bean.

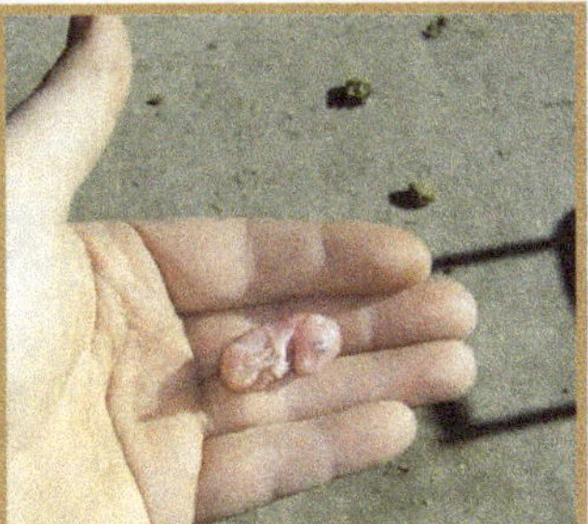

1. Coca-Cola and Pepsi Incident:

In 2006, a Coca-Cola employee tried to sell secrets to Pepsi, which Pepsi reported to Coca-Cola.

2. Hershey's Kisses Name:

Hershey's Kisses were named after the sound of chocolate being deposited.

3. Lego Minifigures:

There are more Lego Minifigures than people on Earth.

4. German Chocolate Cake:

Named after American baker Samuel German, not the country of Germany.

5. Gilberto Baschiera

An Italian banker who secretly redirected funds to poorer clients and avoided jail due to a plea bargain.

6. Apple Land Purchase:

Apple paid a couple $1.7 million for their land, which was worth much less, to build a data center.

 **IKEA Acronym:**

IKEA stands for Ingvar Kamprad Elmtaryd Agunnaryd.

 **Costa Coffee's Gennaro Pelliccia:**

Pelliccia has his tongue insured for £10 million.

 **Pop-up Ads Regret:**

The inventor of pop-up ads regrets creating them.

 **Mirrors Making People Look Thinner:**

Mirrors designed to make people look thinner contribute to 54% of total sales for retailers using them.

 **GIF Patent and PNG:**

The PNG format was created as a free alternative after a patent dispute over GIFs.

 **Hungover as Valid Reason:**

A UK company allows "hungover" as a valid reason for missing work.

 **Cards Against Humanity Black Friday Prank:**

Cards Against Humanity sold a box of bull feces as part of a Black Friday prank, which sold over 30,000 copies.

 **Volkswagen Sausages:**

Volkswagen's currywurst sausages generate more revenue than its cars.

McDonald's Hamburgers:

McDonald's sells 2.5 billion hamburgers annually.

Millionaire Bankruptcy:

Many millionaires face bankruptcy multiple times.

Jobs to China:

The U.S. loses significant jobs to China every year.

Mirrors Making People Look Thinner:

Mirrors designed to make people look thinner contribute to 54% of total sales for retailers using them.

Samsung's Economic Impact:

Samsung's business activities account for more than 15% of South Korea's economy.

Easter Candy Sales:

Americans spend nearly $2 billion on Easter candy each year.

Ripped Dollar Bill:

A ripped dollar bill retains its value if it is larger than half.

McDonald's Visits:

Nine out of ten American children visit McDonald's every month.

Netflix's Marketing Spend:

Netflix spent nothing on marketing its DVD rental service but gained millions of users.

 ## Recessions and Health:

Recessions can improve public health due to reduced pollution and stress.

 ## Restaurant with Grandmas:

A restaurant in New York employs grandmothers instead of chefs.

 ## London Taxi Protest Impact:

Protests by London taxi drivers led to increased use of Uber.

 ## Wacky Laws:

Arizona once had a law against hunting camels, reflecting historical practices.

 ## Soda Tax Impact:

Mexico's sugary drink tax led to decreased consumption of sugary beverages.

 ## Big Mac Index:

The Big Mac Index measures purchasing power parity between countries.

 ## Recycling Industry:

The U.S. recycling industry is worth billions of dollars.

 ## CEO Salaries:

Some CEOs take $1 salaries or receive performance-based compensation.

 ## Hidden Costs of Buying a House:

Buying a house involves numerous hidden costs beyond the purchase price.

 ## Starbucks' Secret Menu:

Starbucks has a popular but unofficial secret menu.

 **Economic Freedom:** Hong Kong has been ranked as having a free economy.

 **Tax-Free Holiday:** Some U.S. states offer tax-free weekends for back-to-school shopping.

 **Zappos' Return Policy:** Zappos is known for its generous return policy.

 **Retail Therapy:** Shopping can provide a temporary mood boost due to dopamine release.

 **Economic Indicators:** Economic indicators assess the health of the economy and guide policies.

 **Product Placement:** Product placement in media is a common advertising strategy.

 **Business Incubators:** Business incubators support startups with resources and mentorship.

 **Frugal Innovations:** Frugal innovation creates affordable solutions for emerging markets.

 **Digital Wallets:** Digital wallets like Apple Pay are transforming payment methods.

 **Advertising Jingles:** Jingles help make products memorable and increase brand recognition.

Diverse Investments:
Investment portfolios include various assets to manage risk.

Economic Sanctions:
Economic sanctions influence the behavior of other nations through trade restrictions.

Retail Data:
Retailers use data analytics for inventory and marketing optimization.

Celebrity Endorsements:
Celebrities endorse products to boost sales and brand recognition.

Microtransactions:
In-game microtransactions contribute significantly to revenue for developers.

Crowdfunding Success:
Crowdfunding platforms help launch successful products and businesses.

Venture Capital:
Venture capital funds startups in exchange for equity.

Global E-commerce:
Online retail sales are projected to reach $6 trillion by 2024.

Corporate Social Responsibility:
Many companies invest in sustainable and ethical practices.

Luxury Brand Resilience:
Luxury brands like Chanel often perform well even during economic downturns.

Price Wars:

Retailers engage in price wars to attract customers and increase market share.

Retail Therapy:

Shopping triggers dopamine release, providing a temporary mood boost.

Economic Indicators:

Indicators such as GDP and unemployment rates assess economic health.

Economic Impact of Tourism:

The global tourism industry contributes over $8 trillion to the world economy.

Microfinancing Impact:

Microfinance institutions help lift millions out of poverty by providing small loans to entrepreneurs.

Brand Value:

The most valuable brand in the world is Apple, with a brand value exceeding $300 billion, as reported by Forbes.

Small Businesses:

Small businesses make up about 90% of businesses worldwide and are crucial for job creation, accounting for more than 50% of global employment.

Startup Success Rate:

Only about 50% of small businesses survive their first five years, and about 30% survive ten years or more, according to the U.S. Small Business Administration.

Gig Economy:

36% of U.S. workers engaged in gig work in 2021.

Global GDP:

Services contribute about 65% to global GDP.

CSR Impact:

Corporate social responsibility boosts employee engagement and loyalty.

Female Entrepreneurs

Women-owned businesses make up 42% of U.S. companies.

Blockchain Impact:

Blockchain will significantly impact the economy by 2025.

Unicorn Startups:

There are over 1,000 unicorn startups worldwide.

Sustainability:

Sustainable companies tend to financially outperform.

Digital Ads:

Digital advertising overtook traditional media in 2019.

Cryptocurrency:

Over 300 million people globally use or own cryptocurrencies.

Global Trade:

International trade has grown significantly, with global trade in goods and services totaling approximately $25 trillion in 2020.

Remote Work:

Up to 70% of the
workforce worked
remotely during
COVID-19.

Brand Loyalty:

Acquiring new
customers is 5
times more
expensive than
retention.

**Wealth
Inequality:**

The top 1%
holds 44% of
global wealth.

Global Inflation:

Inflation has risen
significantly
worldwide.

1. The famous line in Titanic from Leonardo DiCaprio, "I'm king of the world!" was improvised.

2. The Buddha commonly depicted in statues and pictures is a different person entirely. The real Buddha was actually incredibly skinny because of self-deprivation.

3. The first movie ever to put out a motion-picture soundtrack was Snow White and the Seven Dwarfs.

4. **Daniel Radcliffe was allergic to his Harry Potter glasses**: He had an allergy to nickel, and they were quickly replaced with hypoallergenic specs. Also, did you know that his glasses had no lenses? This was to prevent reflections from anything happening behind the scenes. The glass lens was added in post-production.

5. The world's largest grand piano was built by a 15-year-old in New Zealand. The piano is a little over 18 feet long and has 85 keys – 3 short of the standard 88.

6. The lead singer of The Offspring started attending school to achieve a doctorate in molecular biology while still in the band. He graduated in May 2017.

7. The original Star Wars premiered on just 32 screens across the U.S. in 1977. This was to produce buzz as the release widened to more theaters.

8. Violin bows are commonly made from horse hair.

9.   Hanna-Barbera pitched The Flintstones to networks for 8 weeks before it was finally picked up. It became the first-ever animated show to air during primetime.

10.   There is an underwater version of rugby, unsurprisingly called "underwater rugby." It is a contact sport between 2 teams of 6 competing underwater in a pool to score goals while freediving.

11.   Until 2016, the "Happy Birthday" song was not for public use. Meaning that prior to 2016, the song was copyrighted, and you had to pay a license to use it.

12.   I Will Always Love You was originally written and recorded in 1973 by Dolly Parton. It was written as a farewell to her mentor of seven years.

13.   Chicken Run is the highest-grossing stop-motion animated film, even beating The Nightmare Before Christmas.

14.   Popularized by Shakespeare's play, many people think Julius Caesar's last words were, "And you, Brutus?" In reality, he said, "You too, my child?"

15.   By the time they have been retired for 2 years, 78% of former NFL players have gone bankrupt or are under financial stress because of joblessness or divorce.

16.   The popular LMFAO group that created the viral hit, Party Rock Anthem, is made up of an uncle-nephew duo.

17.   Both of the drummers from Queen and Duran Duran had the same name – Roger Taylor.

18.   When Shakira was in second grade, she was rejected by the school choir because her vibrato was too strong. The music teacher told her that she sounded like a goat.

19. **Tennis players can be fined up to $20,000 for swearing while playing at Wimbledon.** It doesn't stop there, though. If players swear once before or during a match, they're fined and given a warning. The second time it happens in one match, they may lose a point. On the third, they may lose a game. Then, finally, they can lose the whole match if they swear four times!

20. **After the premiere of 16 and Pregnant, teen pregnancy rates dropped.** MTV may not have the most wholesome shows, but teen pregnancy dropped by 5.7% within 18 months of the show's premiere. While this sounds like a success story, the TV show has been criticized for glamourizing teenage pregnancy. Instead of focusing on genuine issues, they focus more on the drama between the parents.

21. In the original Psycho movie, the blood in the famous shower scene was actually chocolate syrup.

22. In the film Star Wars Episode Three: Revenge of the Sith, every single one of the Clone Troopers was produced using CGI effects.

23. Aggressive sitting is a sport. It originated in Berlin no later than 2008. You can purchase a special stool for this sport for around 70 dollars.

24. The whole Harry Potter series contains 199 chapters, 4,224 pages, and 1,090,739 words and has been made into 19 hours and 39 minutes of the film.

25. Daniel Radcliffe identifies as Jewish, and his mother is Jewish too.

26. When Jay-Z was 12, he shot his older brother in the shoulder for stealing his jewelry. He later referenced it in a song titled "You Must Love Me."

27. On average, PewDiePie receives around 2 million YouTube views on each video after only 24 hours of uploading them.

28. The first band to ever perform live on all seven continents was Metallica.

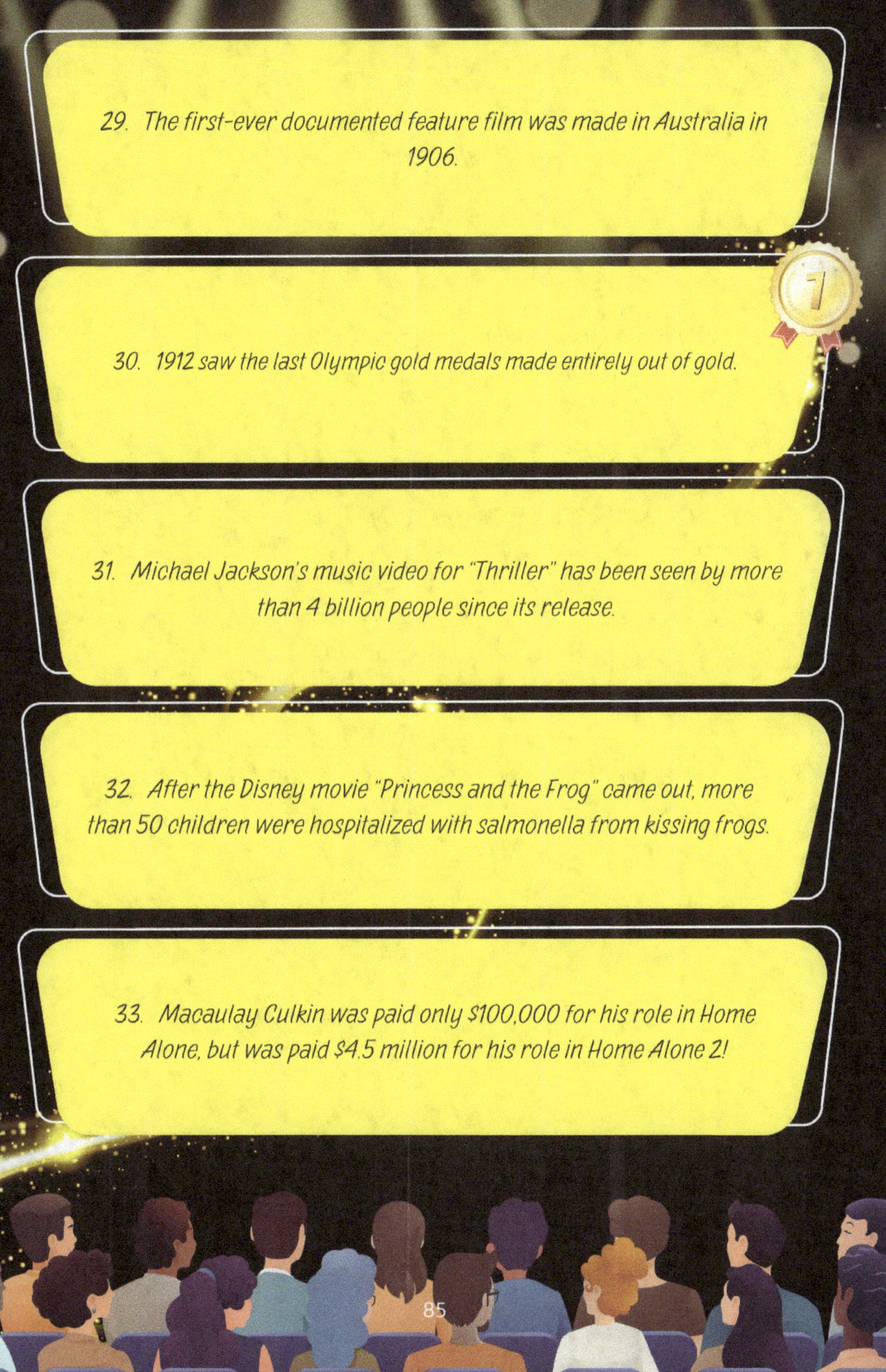

29. The first-ever documented feature film was made in Australia in 1906.

30. 1912 saw the last Olympic gold medals made entirely out of gold.

31. Michael Jackson's music video for "Thriller" has been seen by more than 4 billion people since its release.

32. After the Disney movie "Princess and the Frog" came out, more than 50 children were hospitalized with salmonella from kissing frogs.

33. Macaulay Culkin was paid only $100,000 for his role in Home Alone, but was paid $4.5 million for his role in Home Alone 2!

34. The Power Puff Girls were originally based off of the three good fairies from Sleeping Beauty.

35. Hollywood stars actually sniff powdered vitamin B when you see them sniffing cocaine in the movies.

36. On October 10, 2006, British singer Katie Malua was the first and only record holder for performing a concert 303 meters underwater. Katie and her band performed on Statoil's Troll off the coast of Bergen, Norway. She performed two 30-minute concerts to an audience of oilrig workers. These oil rig workers are the ones who won the ticket to the performance.

37. Believe it or not, the world's shortest song is just 1.316 seconds long! "You Suffer" by Napalm Death is the world's shortest song. Blink and you'll miss it!

38. When was film invented? The 1890s.

39.   The earliest short films were sometimes accompanied by bands.

40.   The Beatles' "Yesterday" is the most covered song in the history of recorded music. Over 2,200 artists have recorded their own versions of it! Talk about leaving a legacy!

41.   The Stradivarius violin is the most expensive musical instrument in the world. It was sold for $16 million in 2011. That's a lot of dough for a fiddle!

42.   The Titanic movie was 17.7 reels long when released.

43.   The Hurrian Hymn No. 6 is the world's oldest song, which is about was sang about 3,400 years ago, making it the oldest song in the history of the world.

44.   The first feature-length film was produced in 1906.

45.   The first movie theaters opened in 1907.

46.   The world's longest concert is currently still ongoing! The concert, which takes place in Halberstadt, Germany, started in 2001 and is planned to end in 2640. That's a whopping 639 years long!

47.   A flute made from a bird bone and mammoth ivory is the oldest known musical instrument in history. It was found in the Swabian Alps in Germany and is estimated to be over 35,000 years old!

48.   *A pool of massive size.* The Citystars Sharm El Sheikh in Egypt is the world's largest swimming pool. If you can believe it, the seawater pool that opened in 2015 measures at over 1 million square feet! The total cost to build a pool that large? A cool $5.5 billion.

49. **What are the four official swimming strokes?** If we're talking about competitive swimming, there are four specific strokes that athletes perform during races. The traditional overhand crawl is called freestyle. The other strokes are backstroke, breaststroke and butterfly stroke. Freestyle is the fastest stroke and breaststroke is the slowest.

50. Jim Carrey was the first actor to star in three consecutive box-office hits.

51. The first rap song to win an Academy Award for Best Original Song was Eminem's "Lose Yourself."

52. **How many people can't swim?** Believe it or not, billions of people around the world can't swim. In fact, it's estimated that over 4 billion people worldwide are unable to stay afloat. This includes almost 60% of Americans. The Red Cross recommends everyone take lessons to learn how to swim because it could save your life.

53. Vincent van Gogh's "The Starry Night" wasn't his most famous work during his lifetime. In fact, Van Gogh only sold one painting while he was alive, and his fame only truly emerged after his death.

54.   Shrek originally had a thick Canadian accent.

55.   There's a soviet version of The Lord of the Rings, and it's downright woeful.

56.   Psy didn't want to upload Gangnam Style to YouTube because he didn't want to be humiliated.

57.   Abercrombie & Fitch once offered the cast of Jersey Shore significant amounts of money to stop wearing their clothes.

58.   The Beatles' song "Yesterday" is the most covered song in history, with over 2,200 recorded versions by different artists since its release in 1965.

59. *Chris Pratt stole his costume from the set of Guardians of the Galaxy.*

60. *Stan Lee created the character for Iron Man as a challenge.*

61. *The directors of the film Despicable Me actually wrote their own language for the Minions called Minionise.*

62. *Film producer Jeffrey Katzenberg revived The Walt Disney Studios by producing some of their biggest hits: The Little Mermaid, The Lion King, Beauty and the Beast, and Aladdin. After these, he requested a promotion and was then abruptly fired by them. He then swore revenge against Disney and founded DreamWorks Studios.*

63. *In the film Star Wars Episode Three: Revenge of the Sith, every single one of the clone troopers was produced using CGI effects.*

64.   Artist Salvador Dalí would often get out of paying for drinks and meals by drawing on the checks, making them priceless works of art and, therefore, un-cashable.

65.   In an interview with Taylor Swift in 2005, she was told, "If music doesn't work out, you could be a hair model." Seven years later, the same woman interviewed her again and apologized for what she said.

66.   Alfred Hitchcock's "Psycho" (1960) was the first American movie to show a flushing toilet on screen. Before this, depicting a toilet in use was considered taboo in Hollywood films.

67.   The Mona Lisa has no eyebrows. This wasn't a stylistic choice by Leonardo da Vinci; rather, over time, the delicate brushstrokes that formed her eyebrows have faded away due to cleaning and restoration efforts.

68.   Bruno Mars's birth name is Peter Gene Bayot Hernandez. His stage name, "Bruno Mars," was inspired by the wrestler Bruno Samartino.

69. The Olympic Games were originally a religious festival held in honor of Zeus, and the first recorded Olympics took place in 776 BC in Olympia, Greece.

70. The song "Bohemian Rhapsody" by Queen was almost not released as a single because record executives thought it was too long (nearly 6 minutes). It went on to become one of the most famous rock songs of all time.

71. The "Happy Birthday" song is one of the most recognized songs in the English language, but it was once copyrighted, and public performances required payment of royalties.

72. Michael Phelps holds the record for the most Olympic gold medals won by any athlete, with a total of 23 gold medals.

73. The movie "Jaws" (1975) was the first film to be widely released in theaters across the United States on the same day, pioneering the modern "blockbuster" release strategy.

1. A single strand of Spaghetti is called a "Spaghetto."

2. Fruit stickers are edible, though the same as any fruit; washing prior to eating is recommended. The glue used for them is regulated by the FDA.

3. Swedish meatballs originated from a recipe King Charles XII brought back from Turkey in the early 1800s.

4. French fries originated in Belgium, NOT France!

5 Studies from Cornell University show that storing apples in a cold environment slows down the ripening process, helping them stay fresh longer.

6 Honey NEVER spoils. Honey found in ancient Egyptian tombs has been found to be still edible due to its natural antibacterial properties.

7 Red wine may contain more antioxidants than white wine. Research indicates that the polyphenols in red wine have higher antioxidant activity compared to white wine.

8 Avocados contain heart-healthy monounsaturated fats. Studies show that the monounsaturated fats in avocados are beneficial for cardiovascular health.

9 Research from Harvard University suggests that the flavonoids in dark chocolate can support cardiovascular health.

10 A study published in the Journal of Neuroscience found that caffeine in coffee can improve memory recall.

11 Toasted bread may contain fewer calories than the original bread.

12 Pasta may have originated in China, NOT Italy. Archaeological evidence suggests that pasta existed in China around 2000 BCE before becoming popular in Italy.

13 Studies show that CHIA SEEDS are a rich plant-based source of Omega-3 fatty acids, even higher than salmon.

14 Coconut water contains potassium, sodium, and electrolytes, making it a good alternative to sports drinks.

15 Studies show that the protein and carbohydrates in milk AID in muscle recovery and REDUCE fatigue after exercise.

16 Different colored vegetables provide various vitamins and minerals. For example, carrots are rich in vitamin A, while tomatoes provide lycopene, a potent antioxidant.

17 Bananas contain tryptophan, an amino acid that helps the body produce serotonin, which supports sleep.

18 Research indicates that catechins in green tea can enhance cognitive function and protect the brain.

19 Studies have shown that ginger can REDUCE nausea and vomiting, especially during pregnancy.

20 Adequate water intake helps maintain digestive health and supports metabolic functions.

21 Probiotics in yogurt help BALANCE gut bacteria and IMPROVE digestive health.

22 Cauliflower is a good source of vitamin C and calcium, contributing to immune function and bone health.

23 Not all popcorn in South Africa is what you think it is. That said, it would be pretty hard for you to not get what you wanted! A local delicacy in some parts of South Africa may taste like popcorn, but it's far from it. This South African "popcorn" is actually termites or ants that have been roasted to crispy perfection!

24 NOT all wine is vegan. With the main ingredient being grapes, you'd think this would be a no-brainer. However, some common ingredients in wine are milk protein, egg white, gelatin, and fish bladder protein.

25 Bad eggs will float. If you need to test the freshness of your eggs, put them in a glass of cold water. The fresher the egg, the faster it will fall to the bottom! Any eggs that float should be thrown out.

26 Ripe cranberries will bounce. If you want to test how ripe your cranberries are, drop them on the ground! Cranberries are nature's bouncy ball – even farmers use this technique to see if their cranberries are ready for shipment!

27 Bird saliva is a delicacy in China.

28 Food is allowed to contain some amount of insects. By FDA standards, there's an allowance for the level of traces of bugs that could be in your food. For example, chocolate can have no more than 60 insect fragments per 100 grams. Peanut butter can't have more than 30 insects per 100 grams.

29 India has the LOWEST meat consumption in the world. Per capita, Indians only consume 7 pounds of meat per person per year.

30 Coffee beans can help eliminate bad breath. If you chew on roasted coffee beans, it can help prevent the bacteria that cause bad breath. Drinking coffee helps too, it's just less effective.

31 Pizza Hut used to be the nation's biggest purchaser of kale. Pizza Hut's salad bar was popular way before kale became a trend back in the early 2010s. They used it as a garnish for its salad bars – it wasn't even for eating!

32 Food tastes different when you're flying. Altitude changes your body chemistry, making certain flavors taste different THAN how they taste when you're on the ground.

33 Coffee is the main source of antioxidants for Americans.

34 Sweet drinks can cause dementia. It's not quite as drastic as it originally sounds. However, studies have shown that people who drink one or more artificially sweetened drinks per day were almost three times more likely to develop dementia.

35 Thomas Jefferson made pasta popular in the U.S. Thomas Jefferson is responsible for bringing the first macaroni machine over to the U.S. after spending time in France. He was also the one who introduced mac and cheese to Americans!

36 Eating carrots can turn your skin orange. Carrots are full of the natural pigment beta-carotene. This pigment is what gives carrots their vibrant orange color. If you eat an excessive amount of carrots, beta-carotene can enter your bloodstream, giving your skin an orange glow! The medical name for this condition is CAROTENEMIA. While it's not one of the best things to have, it's generally harmless.

37 Bananas are curved because they grow towards the sun. Philosophers have pondered the shape of bananas for a long time, arguing until the sun goes down as to why they're curved. Bananas go through a process called "negative geo-tropism." This process causes the fruit to grow upwards toward the sun instead of the ground. This, in turn, gives the banana its familiar curved shape.

38 Most supermarket WASABI is actually horseradish. Real wasabi is challenging to make and expensive. As an alternative, most wasabi for sale is COLORED horseradish with flavorings.

39 One fast-food burger can have meat from 100 different cows. It sounds like a crazy amount, but the ground beef used to make burgers, both in fast food places and grocery stores, is made of a collection of muscle tissues.

40 Crackers have holes in them for a reason. During the baking process, if the crackers have holes in them, it prevents air bubbles from ruining the product.

41 White chocolate ISN'T chocolate. Its name is deceiving because white chocolate DOESN'T have any components of regular chocolate. It's really just a mixture of sugar, milk, vanilla, lecithin, and cocoa butter.

42 49% of Americans over 20 eat a sandwich every day.

43 Popsicles were invented by accident. The details are debated, but the general story is that in 1905, an 11-year-old kid left a mixture of soda and water outside in a cup overnight. It froze, and he ate it in the morning. He originally called it an "Epsicle" (his last name was Epperson). When he later had kids, they started calling it "Pop's Sicle" and the new name was born.

44

In Japan, chefs have to train for over two years in order to qualify to serve pufferfish. Pufferfish is a delicacy in Japan, but if it's prepared wrong, it can kill the person eating it.

45 Spam wasn't invented in Hawaii. Although Hawaii consumed the most Spam per capita than any other state, it was invented in Minnesota. There's even a spam museum in Minnesota!

46 Froot Loops are all the same flavor. As colorful as they are, you'd think they were flavored accordingly! But NO, all Froot Loops are all the same flavor.

47 Expiration dates on bottled water have nothing to do with the water. Water can't expire – but the bottle it's in can. Plastic bottles will eventually start leaking chemicals into the water. It won't make the water harmful to drink, but it will make it taste less fresh.

48 Cheese is the MOST stolen food in the world. In fact, it's stolen so much it has its own percentage! About 4% of all cheese made around the globe ends up stolen. There's even a black market for cheese!

49 Crackers are worse for your teeth than sugar. Acid is the BIGGEST cause of tooth decay, NOT sugar! Crackers tend to stick to your teeth which ends up being a breeding ground for bacteria.

50 Ketchup used to be used as a medicine. Back in the early 1800s, people thought tomatoes had medicinal qualities. One doctor claimed they could treat diarrhea and indigestion, so he made a recipe for a type of tomato ketchup which then became a pill.

51 Nutmeg can act as a hallucinogen if consumed in large quantities. The compound myristicin in nutmeg has psychoactive effects. Ingesting high doses of nutmeg can lead to hallucinations and other symptoms such as dizziness, nausea, and confusion. However, consuming nutmeg in such large amounts can also cause serious side effects and toxicity.

52 Ranch dressing is DYED. One ingredient in ranch is titanium dioxide which is used to make it look whiter. It's the same ingredient that is used in sunscreen and paint for coloring.

53 Strawberries are not berries. Technically, berries only have seeds on the inside, a rule which is obviously broken by strawberries!

54 Serbia hosts the most costly cheese.

55 Potatoes are 80% water. Sure we all know celery is high in water, but who knew potatoes were only 15% behind them! Technically, you could juice a potato, but I don't think anyone wants that.

56 India produces, consumes, and exports the most chili peppers in the world. Chili peppers weren't introduced to India until the 15th century, but they were a hit. These days, they not only eat and grow more than anyone else, but this is where you'll find some of the spiciest peppers such as the bhut jolokia.

57 Turkey consumes the most tea per person.

58 Tonic water glows in the dark. It's weird to think that my insides are glowing whenever I have a gin and tonic, but it's true! Quinine is the component of tonic water which is what causes the glow.

59 There's a small difference between jelly and jam. Jam is made with fruit, which is why it's so chunky. Meanwhile, jelly is made with fruit juice. An easy way to tell the difference between jelly and jam is that jelly will spread evenly, while jam will tend to be a little lumpy.

60 Brown sugar is no different than white sugar. Brown sugar is no less refined than white sugar. The only difference is the fact that some of the molasses that gets removed in the refining process, is added back in.

61 The Netherlands drinks the most coffee per person.

62 Nutritious food is more expensive than junk food. This is a great excuse to use to eat junk food and save money, but our bodies DON'T like it so much! Per ounce, nutritious food costs up to 10 times more than junk food.

63 In an emergency, coconut water can be used for blood plasma. Just like blood plasma, coconut water has levels of high sodium and low potassium. It should only be used in absolute emergencies, because adverse effects may be fever, headaches, itchiness, or aching sensations.

64 Eating fast food regularly has the same impact on the liver as hepatitis.

65 Goat meat is the most popular meat. Although we may be accustomed to burgers, goat meat accounts for 70% of the red meat eaten globally! This is great news because goats are better for you and the environment.

66 Throwing food away is illegal in Seattle.

67 Astronauts ate food grown in space for the first time in 2015.

68 Sound can influence the taste of your food. High-frequency sounds to enhance the sweetness in food, while low frequencies bring out the bitterness.

69 Australians eat the most meat. Coming in at a whopping 200 pounds per person every year, Australians take first place, but are still closely followed by Americans.

70 Hot chocolate tastes better out of an orange cup.

71 Americans eat millions of pounds of peanut butter.

72 Egg yolks are one of the few foods that naturally contain Vitamin D.

73 Avocados have more potassium than bananas. One avocado contains about 975 mg of potassium, while a banana contains about 422 mg.

74 Red wine may be good for your heart. The antioxidants in red wine, particularly resveratrol, have been linked to improved heart health.

75 Peppers have more vitamin C than citrus fruits. Bell peppers, for instance, contain more vitamin C than oranges.

76 Eating spicy food can boost your metabolism. Capsaicin, the compound that makes chili peppers hot, can increase your metabolism and help with weight loss.

77 Cheese comes in thousands of varieties. There are more than 1,000 different types of cheese produced worldwide, each with its own unique flavor and texture.

78 Garlic has been used for its medicinal properties for thousands of years. Garlic has been used in various cultures for its potential health benefits, including its antibacterial and antiviral properties.

79 Olive oil is one of the healthiest cooking oils. Rich in monounsaturated fats and antioxidants, olive oil is associated with numerous health benefits, including improved heart health.

80 Mangoes are rich in vitamin A. Mangoes provide a significant amount of vitamin A, which is essential for good vision, immune function, and skin health.

1. **Arizona Cactus Law:** Cutting down a saguaro cactus in Arizona can be charged as a class-4 felony, potentially resulting in jail time.

2. **Canadians say "sorry" so much** that a law was passed in 2009 declaring that an apology can't be used as evidence of admission to guilt.

3. **Eagle Feather Law:** Only official members of federally recognized Native American tribes may legally possess or collect eagle feathers in the U.S.

4. **50% of apartments in Los Angeles don't come with a fridge.** This is legal, as fridges are considered an "amenity," and therefore, landlords are not required to provide one.

5. In Canada, under Section 11(d) of the Charter, everyone has the right to a fair and impartial trial by an independent jury in criminal cases.

6. In the U.S. state of Georgia, it is illegal to tie a giraffe to a telephone pole or street lamp.

7. It is illegal to play a musical instrument in the Northern Territory, Australia, for the purpose of annoying other people.

8. Arizona fines drivers under their unique "Stupid Motorist Law."

9. In Sweden, it is illegal to name your child "IKEA." Sweden has strict rules about baby names, and the names must not be offensive or likely to cause discomfort to the child.

10. Thailand's Royal Family Law: In Thailand, it is illegal to insult the royal family under the lèse-majesté law. Offenders can face severe penalties, including imprisonment.

11. Russia has laws against the use of foul language in public, with fines imposed for public profanity as part of efforts to maintain public decorum.

12. Germany's Quiet Sundays: In Germany, many activities are restricted on Sundays due to "Ruhetag" laws that promote a quiet day for rest. Most shops are closed, and noise is kept to a minimum

13. United Arab Emirates' Public Behavior Laws: The UAE enforces strict public behavior laws, including regulations against public displays of affection and offensive gestures, to maintain social norms.

14. In the city of Florence, Italy, it is illegal to feed pigeons in the historic city center. This regulation aims to protect the city's historical monuments and public spaces from the damage and mess caused by pigeons.

15. In Greece, there's a mountain that women are prohibited from visiting. Mount Athos in Greece is an autonomous monastic state and is home to a number of Orthodox Christian monasteries. Women are indeed prohibited from visiting Mount Athos, a restriction that has been in place for centuries.

16. China has banned popular social media platforms like Facebook, Instagram, and Twitter.

17. Switzerland's Recycling Rules: Switzerland has some of the strictest recycling laws in the world, with detailed sorting requirements for different types of waste and significant fines for non-compliance.

18. France's Wine Regulations: France has strict regulations governing wine production, including the AOC system (Appellation d'Origine Contrôlée), which ensures quality and authenticity.

19. USA's Legal Drinking Age: The legal drinking age in the U.S. is 21, one of the highest in the world. The law aims to reduce underage drinking and its associated risks.

20. Turkey's Public Holiday for Atatürk: Turkey celebrates April 23rd as National Sovereignty and Children's Day, honoring Mustafa Kemal Atatürk, the founder of modern Turkey, and focusing on children's rights.

21. Singapore's Anti-Littering Laws: Singapore has stringent anti-littering laws with heavy fines for littering, as part of its efforts to maintain cleanliness and order in public spaces.

22. China's One-Child Policy: Implemented from 1979 to 2015, China's one-child policy restricted most families to a single child to control population growth. It has since been replaced with a two-child policy.

23. Sweden's Law on Gender Neutrality: Sweden has implemented gender-neutral policies in various aspects of society, including using gender-neutral pronouns and ensuring equal parental leave.

24. New Zealand Parental Leave Law: New Zealand mandates paid parental leave, ensuring work-life balance for employees.

25. Japan's Apology Law: When a train in Japan leaves the station at the wrong time, the rail company issues a public apology.

26. Germany's Recycling Laws: Germany has some of the strictest recycling laws in the world, with detailed waste sorting requirements.

27. Law and Space Travel: In 1967, the Outer Space Treaty established that space is free for exploration and use by all countries, and that celestial bodies cannot be claimed by any sovereign nation.

28. Royalty and the Law: In the UK, the Queen is immune from prosecution, a unique legal status rooted in the principle of "sovereign immunity."

29. Cheese Protection: In Switzerland, it's illegal to take cheese out of the country without declaring it, due to the nation's strict cheese export laws.

30. Ban on Drones Over Buckingham Palace: Due to security concerns, flying drones over Buckingham Palace is strictly prohibited, with severe penalties for violations.

31. Lie Detector Reliability: While polygraph tests are used in legal settings, their accuracy is debated. Many legal experts consider them unreliable as evidence in court.

32. Art Theft Laws: The 1972 UNESCO Convention protects cultural heritage from theft and illegal trade, reflecting international commitment to preserving global artistic treasures.

33. The Right to Be Forgotten: The EU's "right to be forgotten" law allows individuals to request the removal of outdated or irrelevant personal information from search engine results.

34. Historic Spying Laws: The Espionage Act of 1917 in the U.S. made it a crime to interfere with military operations or support America's enemies during World War I, marking a significant legal development in national security.

35. Bizarre Laws: In Singapore, it's illegal to sell or chew gum, except for therapeutic purposes. This law was introduced in 1992 to combat littering and maintenance issues.

36. Modern Witch Trials: The 1990s "Satanic panic" in the U.S. led to several high-profile trials and accusations of ritual abuse, highlighting how legal systems can be influenced by societal fears and myths.

37. International Law Enforcement: Interpol is an international organization that facilitates cooperation between police forces around the world, enabling them to track and apprehend criminals across borders.

38. Historical Legal Codes: The Code of Hammurabi, one of the oldest known legal codes, was established in ancient Babylon around 1754 BCE and included laws on property, family, and commerce.

39. Privacy Protections: The European Union's General Data Protection Regulation (GDPR) is one of the most stringent privacy laws in the world, protecting the personal data of EU citizens and influencing global data protection practices.

40. Trial by Combat: In medieval Europe, parties in a legal dispute could choose to resolve their issues through a trial by combat, where the victor was considered to have divine favor, thus proving their claim.

41. Maritime Law: Salvage law dictates that if you rescue a ship or its cargo, you're entitled to a reward, but you don't automatically own what you salvage.

42. Fingerprint Evidence: The first criminal conviction using fingerprint evidence was in Argentina in 1892, leading to the widespread adoption of fingerprinting in law enforcement.

43. Mootness Doctrine: In U.S. law, a case can be dismissed if it becomes "moot," meaning there's no longer a dispute to resolve, making the court's decision irrelevant.

44. Statute of Limitations: Most crimes have a statute of limitations, meaning they can only be prosecuted within a certain time frame after the crime is committed. However, there is no statute of limitations for serious crimes like murder in many jurisdictions.

45. Insanity Defense: The first recorded use of the insanity defense was in 1843, in the trial of Daniel M'Naghten, who attempted to assassinate the British Prime Minister. The case led to the establishment of the "M'Naghten Rule," a standard for legal insanity.

50 FACTS ABOUT CULTURE

1

Japan's Ramen Museums: Japan has museums dedicated to ramen, celebrating the history and variety of this iconic dish.

2

Japan's Silence in Elevators: It is considered polite to remain silent in Japanese elevators, as talking loudly is seen as disrespectful.

3

Canada's Thanksgiving Differences: Canadian Thanksgiving is celebrated earlier than in the U.S., focusing on giving thanks for the harvest.

4

Turkey's Tea Time: In Turkey, tea is a significant part of daily life, often enjoyed in social settings.

5

Argentina's Mate Culture: In Argentina, drinking mate is a social activity involving the sharing of the gourd and straw among friends and family.

6

Sweden's Fika Break: Swedes take "fika" breaks, enjoying coffee and pastries with friends, a social institution in the country.

7

India's Holi Festival Colors: During Holi, people throw vibrant powders and water at each other, celebrating the arrival of spring.

8

South Korea's Age Calculation: In South Korea, people traditionally add one year to their age at birth and consider everyone to age together on January 1st.

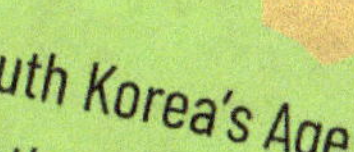

9

Netherlands' King's Day: King's Day is a national holiday in the Netherlands celebrating the king's birthday with street parties and outdoor festivities.

10

China's Confucian Influence: Confucian principles continue to influence Chinese culture, emphasizing respect for elders and social harmony.

11

Iceland's Book Flood Tradition: Iceland's "Jólabókaflóð" is a tradition where books are given as Christmas gifts, and people spend the holidays reading.

12

USA's Super Bowl Sunday: The Super Bowl is a major cultural event in the U.S., with elaborate halftime shows and widespread festivities.

13

Japan's Capsule Hotels: Japan's capsule hotels offer compact sleeping pods, popular for budget-conscious travelers.

14

Nepal's Living Goddess Tradition: In Kathmandu, Nepal, the "Kumari" tradition involves selecting a young girl as a living goddess.

15

Hatsumode in Japan: First shrine visit of the year for good fortune, showing religious influence on New Year traditions.

16

Vesak Festival: Celebrates Buddha's birth, enlightenment, and death in several Buddhist countries.

17

Vietnam's Lunar New Year: Tết Nguyên Đán involves offerings to the Kitchen Gods, blending folk beliefs and religion.

18

Navratri Festival: Hindu festival honoring goddess Durga, showcasing religious-cultural celebrations.

19

Blue Mosque in Turkey: The mosque's design exemplifies the integration of religion and art.

20

Peepal Tree in Hinduism: Venerated as a symbol of life and wisdom, reflecting the religious connection with nature.

21

Finland's Sauna Culture: In Finland, saunas are an integral part of life, with most Finns visiting a sauna at least once a week.

22

USA's Thanksgiving Football Tradition: Watching NFL football games on Thanksgiving is a popular tradition in the United States.

23

Japan's Bowing Etiquette: In Japan, bowing is a common greeting and sign of respect, with different depths and durations depending on the context.

24

Brazil's Samba Dance: Samba is a lively dance originating from Brazil, often associated with Carnival and Brazilian culture.

25

India's Diwali Festival: Diwali, the Festival of Lights, is a major Hindu holiday in India, celebrated with fireworks, decorations, and feasts.

26

New Zealand's Public Holiday for Anzac Day: Anzac Day on April 25th is a national day of remembrance in New Zealand and Australia, honoring military members who served in wars.

27

Ireland's St. Patrick's Day Celebrations: St. Patrick's Day, celebrated on March 17th, is a cultural and religious holiday in Ireland with parades and wearing green.

28

Japan's Cherry Blossom Viewing In Japan, tipping is considered rude, as good service is expected and already included in the experience.

29

Fijian Yaqona Ceremony: In Fiji, the Yaqona (or kava) ceremony is a traditional way of welcoming guests and marking special occasions, involving the sharing of a drink made from the kava root.

30

The Louvre: The Louvre in Paris is the world's largest art museum and a historic monument, housing over 38,000 pieces of art, including the famous Mona Lisa.

31

China's Lantern Festival: The Lantern Festival marks the end of the Chinese New Year celebrations, with people lighting lanterns and enjoying special foods.

32

La Tomatina: La Tomatina, held in Buñol, Spain, is the world's largest food fight, where participants throw overripe tomatoes at each other.

33

Taj Mahal: The Taj Mahal in India was built by Emperor Shah Jahan in memory of his wife Mumtaz Mahal and is considered one of the New Seven Wonders of the World.

34

Greek Mythology: Greek mythology includes a pantheon of gods and goddesses, influencing Western literature and culture.

35

Mardi Gras: Mardi Gras, also known as "Fat Tuesday," is celebrated in New Orleans with parades, music, and masquerade balls, marking the last day of indulgence before Lent.

36

Scottish Bagpipes: Bagpipes are a traditional Scottish instrument, with a history dating back over a thousand years.

37

Russian Matryoshka Dolls: Matryoshka dolls, also known as Russian nesting dolls, consist of a set of wooden dolls of decreasing size placed one inside another, symbolizing motherhood and family.

38

British Afternoon Tea: Afternoon tea became popular in England in the early 19th century, introduced by Anna, Duchess of Bedford.

39

Spanish Paella: Paella is a traditional Spanish dish made with rice, seafood, and saffron.

40

Australian Aboriginal Art: Aboriginal art often uses dot painting and symbolism to convey stories and cultural traditions.

41

Greek Orthodox Easter: Greek Orthodox Easter often involves traditional foods like lamb and Easter bread.

42

Swedish Midsummer: Midsummer is a major celebration in Sweden, marking the summer solstice with dancing and feasting.

43

African Masquerades: Masquerade dances are common in African cultures, often used to celebrate important events and tell stories.

44

Tibetan Prayer Flags: Prayer flags are used in Tibetan culture to promote peace, compassion, and wisdom.

45

Japanese Tea Ceremony: The tea ceremony, or Chanoyu, is a ritualistic preparation and consumption of matcha tea in Japan.

46

Turkish Baths: Traditional Turkish baths, or hammams, offer a communal and relaxing experience.

47

American Thanksgiving: Thanksgiving is an American holiday celebrating harvest and family gatherings with a traditional feast.

48

Dutch Tulip Festival: The Netherlands hosts a tulip festival each spring, showcasing fields of vibrant tulips.

49

Turkish Whirling Dervishes: The Whirling Dervishes perform a spinning dance as a form of meditation and spiritual practice.

50

Swedish Fika: Fika is a Swedish tradition of taking a coffee break with friends or colleagues.

1. **Astronaut:** The word "astronaut" is a compound of the Ancient Greek words "astro," meaning "star," and "naut," meaning "sailor," so it literally means "star sailor."

2. **The name for "robot" has dark origins.** If you look into the etymology of "robot," it comes from the Czech word "robota," which translates to forced labor or work. The word was first used to refer to a fictional humanoid in a play in 1920.

3. **Jesus to Joshua:** Translating "Jesus" from Hebrew to English results in "Joshua." The name "Jesus" evolved through translations from Hebrew to Greek to Latin to English.

4. **Irony Mark:** There is a punctuation mark used to signify irony or sarcasm that looks like a backward question mark ⸮.

5. **Banana Terms:** A cluster of bananas is called a "hand," and a single banana is called a "finger."

6. **Mr. and Mrs. Origins:** The titles Mr. and Mrs. originated from the words "master" and "mistress."

7. **Adjective Order:** To properly write adjectives in order, list them by amount, value, size, temperature, age, shape, color, origin, and material.

8. **Kimono Meaning:** The word "kimono" means a "thing to wear," with "ki" meaning "wear" and "mono" meaning "thing."

9. **Orange Color Origin:** The color orange was named after the fruit. Before oranges arrived in England in the late 15th century, there was no specific word for the color.

10. **Burrito Name:** The word "burrito" means "little donkey" in Spanish. Burritos were first mentioned in a dictionary in 1895, but the reason for the name remains unclear.

11. **Y'all Origin:** The term "y'all" dates back to at least 1631, contrary to the belief that it originated in the 18th or 19th centuries.

12. **Schnapsidee:** "Schnapsidee" is the German word for a ridiculous idea that only sounds good when you're drunk.

13. **Alaska on QWERTY:** Alaska is the only U.S. state that can be typed using only one row of a QWERTY keyboard.

14. **Karaoke's Meaning:** "Karaoke" means "empty orchestra" in Japanese.

15. **Tolkien's Languages:** J. R. R. Tolkien invented the languages of Middle Earth before he wrote stories in the fictional universe.

16. **Quarantine Origin:** The word "quarantine" comes from the Venetian dialect of Italian, "quaranta giorni," meaning "forty days."

17. **Longest Alphabetical Word:** The word "almost" is the longest word in English with its letters in alphabetical order.

18. **Deadline Origin:** The term "deadline" originated during the American Civil War, where a line in the dirt marked the boundary for prisoners.

19. **Fly Off the Handle:** The phrase "fly off the handle" originates from the 1800s, referring to the handle of a tool coming off due to misuse.

20. **Velociraptor Meaning:** "Velociraptor" comes from Latin, with "velox" meaning swift and "raptor" meaning robber.

21. **Bi-weekly Definitions:** The term "bi-weekly" can mean either twice a week or once every two weeks.

22. **Dord:** Webster's Dictionary accidentally included the non-existent word "Dord" for five years.

23. **Longest Word Without Vowel:** The longest English word without a vowel is "rhythms."

24. **OK Origin:** The term "OK" originated from a humorous misspelling of "all correct" as "oll korrect" in the 1830s.

25. **Palindrome:** A palindrome reads the same backward as forward, such as "madam" or "racecar."

26. **Pangram:** A pangram uses every letter of the alphabet at least once, like "The quick brown fox jumps over the lazy dog."

27. **Nice Etymology:** The word "nice" originally meant "foolish" or "silly" in Middle English.

28. **Language Diversity:** Approximately 7,000 languages are spoken around the world today.

29. **Shakespeare's Contributions:** William Shakespeare coined over 1,700 words and phrases, including "eyeball" and "bedroom."

30. **Tomato Pronunciations:** The word "tomato" has different pronunciations worldwide, such as "tuh-MAH-toh" and "tuh-MAY-toh."

31. **Set Meanings:** The word "set" has over 430 different meanings in the Oxford English Dictionary.

32. **Word Stress:** Stress on different syllables can change the meaning of words, like "record" as a noun or verb.

33. **Hello Origin:** The word "hello" was popularized by Thomas Edison for telephone greetings.

34. **Alphabet Origin:** The word "alphabet" comes from the first two letters of the Greek alphabet: alpha and beta.

35. **Uncopyrightable:** "Uncopyrightable" is the longest English word that can be written without repeating any letters.

36. **Most Common Letter:** The most frequently used letter in English is "e," making up about 13% of written texts.

37. **Anagram Fun:** The word "listen" is an anagram of "silent," meaning they use the same letters in different orders.

38. **Blue Color Name:** The color name "blue" was not used in ancient languages and was often lumped with other colors.

39. **Smallest Alphabet:** The Rotokas language of Papua New Guinea has one of the smallest alphabets, with only 12 letters.

40. **Gadget Origin:** "Gadget" likely comes from the French "gadget," meaning a small mechanical device.

41. **Bookkeeper:** "Bookkeeper" is one of the few unhyphenated English words with three consecutive double letters.

42. **Screeched:** "Screeched" is often cited as the longest single-syllable word in English.

43. **Eye Pronunciation:** The word "eye" is pronounced differently in different contexts, adding to its playful nature.

44. **Book Origin:** The word "book" comes from Old English "bōc," related to the word "beech" because early books were written on beech wood tablets.

45. **English Word Count:** Estimates suggest over 170,000 words are currently in use in the English language.

46. **Nerd Coined by Dr. Seuss:** The term "nerd" was coined by Dr. Seuss in his 1950 book "If I Ran the Zoo."

47. **Inuit Snow Words:** The Inuit languages have multiple words for snow, though this is nuanced and complex.

48. **Typewriter:** The word "typewriter" can be typed using only the top row of keys on a QWERTY keyboard.

49. The Japanese term for a Shotgun Wedding is "Dekichatta kekkon," which literally translates to "oops-we-did-it-marriage."

CONCLUSION

 s we reach the end of this journey through 999 fascinating facts, I hope you've enjoyed discovering the myriad of intriguing tidbits that make our world so wonderfully complex. Whether you've found yourself enlightened by a peculiar historical detail, amused by an unexpected scientific truth, or inspired by an obscure piece of trivia, these facts are meant to spark curiosity and enrich your conversations.

Remember, knowledge is a powerful tool that can both win arguments and add a touch of brilliance to your interactions. Use these facts wisely, and don't be afraid to share them with enthusiasm—they just might be the key to a compelling discussion or a memorable moment of connection.

In conversations and debates, these facts can serve as powerful tools to illuminate points, challenge assumptions, and, perhaps, even win over skeptics. However, remember that the true joy of sharing knowledge lies not just in the victory of an argument but in the shared wonder and discovery that come with learning something new.

I encourage you to continue exploring, questioning, and seeking out new facts and insights. The world is full of wonders waiting to be uncovered, and your journey of discovery does not end here. Embrace the joy of learning and the thrill of sharing fascinating tidbits with those around you.

Thank you for joining me in this exploration of the remarkable and the whimsical. May your newfound knowledge bring you both intellectual satisfaction and delightful conversations. Here's to continuing the quest for knowledge and to the many exciting discoveries that lie ahead!